Ben Robertson is a former journalist with the *Courier-Mail*, *Sunday Mail* and WIN Television. He is the author of *The Von: Stories and Suggestions from Australian Golf's Little Master* (UQP 1999), *The Second Father: An Insider's Story of Cops, Crime and Corruption* (UQP 2009), and *The People's University* (UQP 2010), the centenary history of the University of Queensland.

BEN ROBERTSON

HEAR ME ROAR

THE STORY OF A STAY-AT-HOME DAD

UQP

First published 2012 by University of Queensland Press
PO Box 6042, St Lucia, Queensland 4067 Australia

www.uqp.com.au
uqp@uqp.uq.edu.au

Cataloguing-in-Publication entry is available
from the National Library of Australia
http://catalogue.nla.gov.au/

978 0 7022 3886 4 (pbk)
978 0 7022 4677 7 (ePub)
978 0 7022 4676 0 (ePDF)
978 0 7022 4678 4 (kindle)

Typeset in 12/18 pt Bembo by Post Pre-press Group, Brisbane
Printed in Australia by McPherson's Printing Group

University of Queensland Press uses papers that are natural, renewable
and recyclable products made from wood grown in sustainable
forests. The logging and manufacturing processes conform to
the environmental regulations of the country of origin.

The author has changed the names of some characters in this memoir;
other characters are composites of a couple of people. This has been
done to protect their privacy.

For Darlene

Sometimes the road less travelled is less travelled for a reason.

Jerry Seinfeld

PROLOGUE

Maybe, just maybe, all this tiredness and confusion is due to the drugs.

'Things might get worse before they get better,' the GP warns as the printer beside her spits out the script. I don't know what better is anymore so this must be the part where I get worse.

I read that John Lennon struggled with loneliness when he was a stay-at-home dad. He told Yoko he wanted to talk to other house husbands about the suffocating isolation, about the mood swings and the depression. But Yoko said he couldn't find anyone. I hadn't known before then that John Lennon was a trailblazer for stay-at-home dads, that he was changing nappies on the frontline in the seventies, years before *Mr Mom* became a hit movie.

Sometimes when I collapse into bed of an evening I dream about writing songs and baking bread with John Lennon at our specially convened fathers' playgroup. My toddler Fergus is playing contentedly with his son Sean. I'm strumming a guitar (and I don't play the guitar so it must be a dream), stopping to give my baby Henry his bottle of formula.

John sips on a cup of green tea as I pour out my heart about the pressures of fatherhood and the difficulties of being stuck in the house. I talk to him about the effects of the medication, about the anxiety and the anger. I talk to him about my father. He nods sagely.

'Don't worry, you're not going crazy,' John says. 'You're a good dad.'

He's the only one who understands.

1

HELLO, LITTLE MAN

I met her at the Mad Cow.

Townsville in North Queensland – home of the Lavarack Barracks, the rugby league team the Cowboys and a mosquito-borne disease called Ross River fever – isn't the world's most romantic city, although I would tell Andy and Nick, all gooey voiced over the phone, that the girl of my dreams had stolen my heart in one of the nightclubs that line Flinders Street. In truth, the beer-and-rum soaked Mad Cow tavern with its black-and-white façade, udder bar and saloon-style décor was a great place to get into a fight on a Friday night or, it would seem, to fall in love.

'She was walking in and I was walking out,' I'd said. 'A few seconds either way and we would never have met.' Nick told me later that when I talked about Darlene I made Townsville sound like some kind of *Casablanca*.

'I've been to Townsville,' he said. 'It's a shithole.'

As I rub my fingers through her long curly brown hair I think about fate and destiny, those precious seconds. What if I'd stayed home that night like I'd originally planned? What if we'd never bumped into each other? Would I have still found her? If I hadn't challenged her to a dancing competition on the Mad Cow dance floor Darlene wouldn't be lying on the operating table at the Mater Mothers' Hospital, the lower half of her body anaesthetised in preparation for the birth of our first child. Right now, there is in me an overwhelming love for her, a love that seems magnified under the bright warm lights of this theatre.

I thought I would never see a more breathtaking sight than when she walked down the aisle at our garden wedding on the Sunshine Coast, dressed in a glittering white Darb dress and smelling of the fresh lotus flowers she held by long green stems in her hand. But how beautiful she looks here, prepped for surgery, so vulnerable and terrified and in need of protection. More than ever, she needs me, reaching out so that I can hold and squeeze her hand, and that makes her stunning.

We planned on a natural birth and had attended prenatal classes where our names, written on tags in thick Nikko pen, were stuck on our chests before we participated in the group sessions with other equally nervous first-time parents. We played a sort of pregnancy version of Trivial Pursuit, practised holding a plastic dummy baby, and were given a tour of the birthing suites and accommodation for new mums when the big day arrived. At the end the lights were dimmed and we watched a film that showed a young couple having a baby.

It wasn't as gory as the film I'd seen on the projector in biology class back at the Catholic boys' school I'd gone to in Brisbane in the 1980s. In that film a woman with gigantic pale breasts had wailed and screamed. The impossible contortions of her spectacularly hairy and swollen vagina were followed by an enormous gush of blood between her splayed legs, which made my head swim . . . not to mention that the doctor nearly dropped the bluish baby that popped out at the same time, almost like he was juggling a tricky catch at first slip. What followed was even worse: a dinner-plate sized placenta, all reddish-blue with bulging veins and vessels, that had us squirming in our plastic seats and discussing at big lunch how it reminded us of *Alien* when John Hurt gave birth to that nasty extraterrestrial. But then the Christian Brothers probably knew that such graphic images (from the biology film, not *Alien*) would be enough to either swear us to celibacy and maybe into the priesthood or to abstain from sex until we were well and truly married and committed to seeing such horrors through to their time-consuming and financially draining aftermath. I'd sat there wide-eyed and just giggled when our biology teacher explained why the mother in the film had such large nipples, so enormous in fact they looked as though someone had knocked over a pot of ink on white writing paper.

'Could you please tell the class why you think the word *nipple* is so funny, Mr Robertson.'

'I don't think it's funny, Miss.'

'Then say it for me will you, Mr Robertson. *Nipple.*'

'Nipple,' I said, and Andy and Nick laughed through their covered mouths, and I laughed, too, and ended up in the form master's office.

The film at the Mater Mothers' Hospital focused more on the role of the politically correct titled 'support person', and the things that could be done to make the pregnant woman happy before she went into battle. The support person in the film was called Ken – he may have been her husband or he may have been her boyfriend or he may have been just a support person, we'll never know. He was rubbing his partner's lower back with a tennis ball, getting cloths to wipe her brow and helping her with her breathing as he gently eased her through the pain with kind words of encouragement. It seemed to me that Ken was a real superhero, the star of the film, which didn't seem right as he was stealing all the glory from the mother, and where was all that gore we'd been brainwashed with back at school?

Afterwards, when the lights were turned back on, the midwife asked if anyone had any questions.

'Can I get Ken's phone number?' asked a young father-to-be with an Irish accent who'd been making everyone laugh all day. 'I think he will do a much better job than me.'

Unfortunately the natural birth Darlene so desperately wanted never eventuated because at the due date there were medical complications and a Caesarean was recommended.

The baby was breech – wrong way up in the womb with its head wedged uncomfortably under her breasts. The obstetrician said we could go ahead with a natural birth if we wanted to but the risks to the baby and to Darlene were high.

'Things could get tricky, but I've delivered hundreds of breech babies,' he said. We liked the obstetrician. He was old and wise, from a time when expectant mothers seemed to be not nearly as tense and certainly didn't have nearly as many questions learned from hours searching the internet. We trusted him. Despite his confidence, though, we could tell by the subtle undertones in his voice that a caesar was definitely the best option. But he wasn't going to push us. It would be our decision.

When Darlene first visited him at his consulting rooms in the city he told her not to become a crack addict or to go bungy jumping, but she could do everything else. She asked about a bacterial disease called Listeria infection that could affect pregnant women; whether she should avoid soft cheeses, eggs and processed foods.

'For goodness sake, just relax and enjoy yourself,' he said. 'Use your common sense. You can even have a glass of wine every now and then if you feel like it.' That's exactly what we were after from a doctor. With so much information available there was a tendency to over-analyse everything.

'You're having a very boring pregnancy,' he used to say to Darlene, which was his way of putting us at ease. Everything was going to be okay. We still thought about going through with it and having a natural birth but then considered a story someone had told us about a family friend who'd lost her breech baby in the delivery room. As long as the baby and Darlene were healthy, we decided we didn't care how it came out.

I had been a Ken-of-sorts up until now. I'd rubbed her belly with cocoa butter, fed her Subway foot-long salad and chicken rolls (no olives or carrot) and her favourite green chicken curries from the local Thai restaurant, massaged her swollen feet and coped with wild mood swings when she would be bright and bubbly one second then threatening to strangle me the next. One night she burst into tears before a movie on television had even started.

'I know I'm going to cry later so I'm going to cry now,' she said in response to my concerned look. She cried again during a commercial for the Commonwealth Bank. 'The family in that ad is just so gorgeous.'

Another time she started laughing at the dinner table and wouldn't stop. Then, not ten minutes later, she had the tissues out telling me how sick she was of feeling like a beach ball.

'I'm fat, fat, fat . . . disgusting and fat.'

Despite all this madness, I thought we were ready. Darlene had churned through a mountain of books on the birthing process and what might follow. We'd watched soothing DVDs narrated by plum-voiced British experts called Miriam. Only when it was over did I realise how far from ready we really were.

★

The Rolling Stones' 'Satisfaction', is playing in the background from another room or over a loudspeaker; I'm not sure where it's coming from. The bearded and middle-aged anaesthetist sings and hums along under his breath, 'I can't get no . . . satisfaction . . . hey hey hey . . .' as he threads the needle into the epidural space around her spinal cord. Darlene starts to shake uncontrollably and complains of the cold, a side effect when the drugs used to numb the nerves are injected into her lower back. There is a chance of paralysis, the anaesthetist had said, or a clot developing that could lead to complications, maybe travelling into her brain and killing her. A percentage was given to that risk.

After nine months I had grown weary of being given risk percentages. At the beginning there was Down syndrome, spina bifida and other conditions that kept me up at night with worry. And then we were told that even if everything looked good at the birth there was still a possibility of blindness, deafness, sudden infant death syndrome and autism. *There's a two per cent chance of this! Depending on your age a one-in-500 chance of that!* I had given up reading the baby books Darlene enjoyed so much because they scared the hell out of me.

'You're not interested in this baby,' she had said on occasions when her hormones were running wild. There was too much information about what could go wrong. I just wanted to focus on what might go right. And then there was my father, always in the back of my mind.

We had not bothered doing the test for Down syndrome, which involved an injection into the uterus that might kill the foetus (another percentage of risk). And even if the baby did have Down syndrome, what then? Now that I had seen the ultrasound, seen its heart beating, seen its tiny arms and legs moving, how could we terminate it? Nick's younger brother had Down syndrome. He was the ultimate optimist who loved taking around the bucket of water we washed our mouthguards in at rugby training, and handing out the cut-up oranges at half-time. It seemed ludicrous that anybody would have wanted to terminate him, this person who so much enjoyed every detail of life and made everyone around him happy.

Despite my relatively strict Catholic upbringing I am not overly religious and had long ago dispensed with Sunday Mass, but we agreed to 'take the hand that God has dealt us' because that seemed like the best way to explain it when people asked if we had done the amniocentesis test that women aged in their mid-thirties sometimes take. Thanks to computers everyone is so much better informed now. Sometimes I wonder if the fathers of years past had it better, men like my dad who sat it out in a waiting room and slapped each other on the back, maybe smoked a cigar, when the news came through. Ignorance must have been bliss, although not being there for the birth is something I wouldn't have missed for anything.

I am tapped on the shoulder by one of the male nurses who is starting to take photos with the digital camera I have provided him. It is the Kodak moment of all Kodak moments, more important than the wedding, which I never thought possible. There is a clean blue sheet, the same colour as the rather comical gown and shower cap I've been given to wear, held in place on a frame over my wife's chest so I cannot see the obstetrician cutting her open, and it is now time for me to stand up and see my firstborn son emerging from the womb.

It is a moment that is impossible to prepare for, not at all what I was expecting. I had imagined her panting and sweating, just like in a Hollywood movie, as I rubbed her shoulders and back, bursting into tears when the baby popped out. There is none of this, no overwhelming feeling of joy, or tears, or tenderness, nothing like what I feel for my wife who is clearly in distress as she is tugged and pulled in every direction as the baby is yanked free. Every one of my senses is on high alert; the smells, the sights, the sounds, all bombard my brain, vying for attention, demanding to be the one that will be remembered is the years that follow. Here's what I will remember, though: the obstetrician and his assistant laughing.

Whatever tension there has been in the operating theatre, it is broken by a remarkable moment because the baby – my baby, our baby – has just crapped all over both surgeons, splattering their chests with a greenish black tar-like substance that I remember from the lectures is called meconium. The obstetrician's pale blue eyes twinkle from the gap between his mask and cap. He has my baby by one leg, the other spread-eagled at an impossible right angle due, I find out later, to his cramped position in the womb – there was a danger, we'd been warned, that because he hadn't turned properly he might have dislocated hips. The baby is dangled before me, covered in blood and yellow mucus and squealing.

'Here's a photo for his twenty-first,' the obstetrician says as the flash goes off.

A moment of incredible tunnel vision overwhelms me as I zero in on the baby's left ear. It is *my* left ear, slightly wrinkled and speckled with blood, but a tiny exact replica nonetheless. This is definitely not the milkman's kid. My God, I think, I am a father and this is my child, a child who possesses my left ear. How truly incredible!

I thought I already knew my baby quite well from the ultrasounds and the tummy rubs when I felt him kick and squirm as I'd sung and read stories to him, my wife lying with her feet up on the couch or propped up with pillows in our double bed. The ear brings on a moment of panic. This is happening, this is serious – I am a father.

I've always been like this. There needs to be visual concrete evidence or at the very least a firm image in my mind before I can get excited, before I can truly commit or believe. I couldn't picture myself being a father. What did I know of being a father anyway? My relationship with my father was a complicated disaster. Estranged since my parents' divorce, I haven't spoken to him in years. He doesn't even know that I'm having a baby, that as of a few seconds ago he is a grandfather. All I know is that I so desperately want to be a better father than he was or is; to provide the love and trust and security and confidence in my child that he never could me. And now there is this blood-spattered left ear, and I anchor on to it.

We already knew he was going to be a boy. We agreed that the birth would be exciting enough and that knowing the sex wouldn't detract from the experience. In this regard we were definitely in the minority, with most of the people we knew astonished at our disregard for tradition. Nick, as usual, put it best: 'I bet you open your presents before Christmas.' Our baby was already named too, which I found out later is bad luck in some cultures but then I am not one for superstitions and neither is Darlene. I've always believed that bad luck and good luck are dished out in equal measure. If the vagaries of life are controlled by such things as walking under ladders or shattered mirrors or naming babies before they are born then we are all in a lot more trouble than we bargained for. As we both came from Scottish and Irish stock Darlene and I had agreed without the slightest hint of argument on the name Fergus. It was a strong Celtic name meaning 'man of strength'. Knowing he was a boy had apparently also made it easy for everyone at the baby shower. My wife told me they didn't have to buy neutral yellow for baby clothes. I had lived my whole life up till this point blissfully unaware that yellow was the Switzerland of baby colours.

The size of his swollen scrotum takes me by surprise. I guess I wasn't listening to the midwife in the prenatal classes because this is perfectly normal in newborns it turns out, due to the hormones.

'His nuts, look at the size of his nuts,' I think. Although I did not think it, as Darlene told me later that I shouted it out loud enough for the whole ward to hear, and the nurses and doctors laughed.

Those few seconds since he was pulled from the womb seemed to take an eternity, like we were all moving sluggishly through the final part of a wonderful dream, but then everything happened quickly after that. The doctors and nurses and hospital orderlies did their jobs efficiently and expertly, with a minimum of fuss. A child is born, but for them it is business as usual, knowing that after we leave another woman will be wheeled in and the process repeated, another caesar, another operation. New actors would be added to the drama but the supporting cast will remain the same. Nevertheless, at this moment when time has almost stood still, there is great joy in the theatre, everyone is happy; a new healthy life has entered the world and its presence and energy demand attention.

While the doctor sews up my wife I am ushered to a side table to cut the umbilical cord. I hold the scissors awkwardly and try to snip through the cord but it is much harder than I would have ever imagined. I have to readjust my grip to finish the job. I am reminded of a piece of calamari as I cut through it, for it is tough and rubbery and I am terrified the scissors will slip, opening up a horrible wound across my son's belly, which looks as thin as tissue paper. Now that the baby has been cleaned up he is taken over to his mother. Fergus is making a strange squawking sound, crying for her, his eyes closed, his hands reaching out, grasping.

'Here you go, Mum,' the elderly nurse says. 'Here's your son.' Darlene cries as her baby cuddles into her, tears spilling down her face. It is both moving and tragic for she wants to sit up and hold him properly, put him to her engorged breast, but because of the ongoing operation she has to let him go after a minute so the paediatrician can check him over.

'You're a mother,' I tell her, trying to ease her distress, tasting the salt on her cheeks as I kiss her again and again. 'You did so well.'

'You're a daddy,' she sobs.

I am taken to another room where Fergus is weighed and measured and poked and prodded. The paediatrician, a small nimble man with freckles and a confident laugh, conducts a thorough evaluation.

'His hips are fine,' the paediatrician tells me. 'Ten fingers, ten toes. All good.'

'His breathing sounds weird,' I say.

'Yes, his lungs still have some amniotic fluid.'

'Is that serious?'

'It's nothing to worry about, perfectly normal in caesar babies. The fluid would normally be squeezed out in a natural birth.'

I look for signs of panic in the paediatrician's face and voice although I can detect nothing. Doctors are like pilots. Even with disaster approaching they remain poker-faced. I still don't believe him.

'We'll have to put him in a humidicrib for a while, though,' the paediatrician continues calmly. 'Just to be sure.' At that moment I finally understand what it means to be a parent because I would gladly give my life for the health of this child. It is all that matters, this little seven-pound bundle that I've only just met but would gladly swap places with.

Fergus is wheeled in a trolley to another larger room where nurses are bustling around other infants in humidi-cribs. On the way there our trolley passes a nurse walking in the opposite direction who hears him cry and says, 'Oh, another caesar baby.'

'These people are incredible experts,' I think, 'to be able to deduce such information from a mere cry.' It is a week till Christmas and the caesar birthrate storms relentlessly upwards. No one, it seems, wants to subject their baby to a Christmas birthday; either that or the obstetricians want to get away early for their holidays at the beach. The nurse tells me to keep a close eye on my baby and to call her over if I need her help. Spinning through my mind are images of blue lips, convulsions, death gasps, of not properly seeing the warning signs.

'I don't want you to go,' I say to the nurse.

'It's going to be okay,' she says kindly. 'He'll be fine, it's just a precaution.'

It is just the two of us, father and son, and I hold out my index finger for Fergus to clutch. I would like to say something profound to him because it seems like such a complete moment, quote a line from Tennyson or Shakespeare about the love flooding my heart: 'One half of me is yours, the other half yours – mine own,' I would say, 'but if mine, then yours. And so all is yours.' But all I can come up with are clichés, 'Hello, little man. Hello, hello.'

Darlene is wheeled in a short time later, still lying on her back. She is crying because she wants to hold Fergus but he is in the humidicrib, on his chest, cheek to the side, fingers opening and closing, still squawking. The obstetrician comes in and tells us the operation has been a success. He touches Darlene on the shoulder lightly, the gesture of a man who cares.

'A great result, Mum,' he says. 'Well done.' Darlene has been hooked up with a catheter, still unable to move from the waist down due to the sedative. Her face looks puffy from the drugs and the high emotion.

'And finally, congratulations, Dad,' the doctor says turning to me happily, shaking my hand vigorously before walking away, whistling a little tune. Oh the joy of bringing life into the world, I think. What a lucky bastard to have such a job. But then it occurs to me that there would be days when things don't go right. With new life, death must also lurk around the corner, waiting patiently for its grim opportunity.

A friend of Andy's lost their baby when there was 'an accident with the forceps'. It sounded so awful that I didn't question further as to what that actually meant, picturing a big pair of metal prongs slipping on wet soft flesh and bone. What does the obstetrician say to those fathers when things have not turned out well, especially when there has been an accident with the forceps? I think back to that film in biology class and how the doctor nearly dropped the baby as it shot out. It's a pretty sure bet that a doctor somewhere in the world has dropped a baby or two in their time. If a member of the Australian cricket team can be castigated for dropping a catch, what recriminations await a doctor who can't hold onto a baby when the game is on the line? And why am I even thinking about stuff like this? I'm not usually a glass-half-empty kind of guy.

The nurse comes over again and hands Fergus to his mother. 'But only for a minute or two, okay,' she says. Darlene cuddles Fergus and starts crying again.

'Hello, beautiful,' she whispers. 'What a handsome little man.'

'I love you,' I whisper to her, leaning down.

'I love you too,' she replies.

Then in an awkward, hurried movement she quickly hands Fergus over to me and dry retches into a bedpan.

2

CLUELESS PARENTS

It is after midnight and Fergus is fast asleep in his white hand-woven cane bassinet, the same one I had slept in as a newborn back in the late sixties. My sister, Kylie, and two brothers, Colin and Daniel, had been lugged around in it too, as had Kylie's four kids. A lady from a baby shop in Fortitude Valley told me that retro pieces like ours were fetching a small fortune for their lucky owners . . . *they don't make them like that anymore* . . . and perhaps we should think about selling it on eBay or maybe to her when we had finished with it. She was looking at the bassinet greedily when we took it in to get a mattress fitted, licking her thin red lips. I told her – in not so many words and much more eloquently – that the sale of such a valued family heirloom would be followed by the removal of my testicles by my mother and sister armed with large knives. Kylie never throws anything out that has historical importance to the family, especially anything to do with her children – she even kept the pegs used on their belly buttons when the umbilical cord was cut and is thinking about having the bassinet mounted and put on permanent display in a corner of her home. It was all I could do to wrestle it out of her clutches.

It comforted me to know that Fergus is safe and secure inside this bassinet, just as I had been when I was small and helpless, just as we all had been. But my wife is not safe and secure. At first I think the muffled whimpering is coming from Fergus during a late-night breastfeed because Darlene sometimes feeds him while propped up by pillows in our bed, but when I reach out for her in the dark, the sheets are warm and empty. And then I hear the water running in the ensuite, look at the late hour on the alarm clock and go to investigate. Darlene is trying to ease the excruciating pain in her breasts, sitting cross-legged on the stone tiles, letting the hot water run over her. The dreaded mastitis is back.

'You've got to help me,' she says. She looks more distressed than I've ever seen her. My wife is tough, carrying a baby around for nine months is proof of that, but the pain this time seems to overwhelm her. I drag a chair over to the glass shower door and reach in, rubbing the swollen glands of their blockages, slowly and carefully, just like the midwife at the

Mater Mothers' Hospital had shown me when it first started. Ken would have been proud.

Even though it is late I am more than glad for the opportunity to help out as in a lot of ways, apart from changing nappies, giving baths and washing clothes, there isn't a hell of a lot I can do on a more intimate level for Darlene while Fergus is still being breastfed. She certainly doesn't want me coming anywhere near her breasts in a sexual way. In fact, she doesn't want me coming anywhere near her in a sexual way, full stop. Unlike men from my father's generation, from the time my son is born I have had a front row seat to the secret world of women and babies. Like most blokes my age, I feel privileged to be given this seat – in fact, we demand it nowadays – although I'm starting to suspect my father's generation and those before him probably had it the right way around.

When it came to witnessing the gory and painful secrets of the gentler sex, up until a certain point in our culture it had all been played out discreetly behind closed doors. I'd never even heard of mastitis before; it certainly wasn't something discussed in the rugby change rooms. When I was growing up I even remember arguing with Andy in kindergarten about whether the queen actually took a dump or not. I couldn't imagine a beautiful delicate creature such as my mother doing something like this, and the queen would be no different. And, if women did engage in such things, I thought they would have to emerge from the toilet with a perfect package wrapped in a red ribbon, smelling like lavender or roses, to be deposited discreetly in the nearest receptacle. I certainly didn't have the courage or the bad manners to ask Mum if *she* ever took a dump. It was only when I saw our pretty teenage babysitter sitting on the toilet with her pants around her ankles while a foul smell wafted to my nostrils that I realised I'd been living in fairyland. Another much older babysitter had convinced me that the farting sound she made when she walked down the steps into the kitchen came from her squeaky shoes. I believed her then, but now I know everything there is to know about the fairer sex – or do I?

After the birth, just when I thought I'd seen everything there was to see, I was sent out on an emergency dash to Sally's house to pick up a set of plastic nipple guards. Fergus was tearing Darlene's boobs to shreds. Every time she fed him, which seemed to be every second of the day, she grimaced and clenched her teeth as if a stapling gun had been triggered on her chest. Sally, Andy's wife, laughed at me when she gave me the nipple guards, her nipple guards to be precise, which looked like mini basketball hoops attached to a thick mesh. I studied them suspiciously as I rolled them around in my hands. *How will these help?*

'It's for air circulation, to stop her clothes from rubbing against her,' said Sally.

'Against her nipples?'

'Of course against her nipples, you idiot.'

There was a time when I would never have believed all the leaking and cracking and bleeding that came with babies and breastfeeding, not to mention the frustration. But then the real story wouldn't have sat very well with that Doris Day image of women I'd grown up with in my younger years – right up until that biology class, that is – of the baby coming out all perfect and clean, and everything so sweet and easy. Even now, with all the gritty realism on television and at the movies, I can't imagine a producer pitching Angelina Jolie with mastitis and nipple guards to Warner Bros. When Fergus was born it took nearly a day for him to latch on and feed. And he wanted to feed, opening and closing his mouth, grabbing at Darlene's chest and hair to get a grip. He seemed so helpless. I felt helpless too.

Standing there watching anxiously from a corner of the room, I couldn't see what sort of evolutionary purpose this difficulty in breastfeeding might serve, other than to completely decimate our species. *Feed, goddamn it, feed.* How is it that we humans continue to thrive when breastfeeding was, for the most part, so difficult and clumsy? I couldn't understand it. In the David Attenborough documentaries I've always liked watching on television, the first thing baby animals did on the grassy savannah when they came out of the womb was struggle to their feet. That little giraffe, wobbling on his long legs, was cactus if he didn't get up and feed as lions and hyenas would soon be circling, looking for signs of weakness.

Children were being breastfed during the Blitz when London was bombed in the Second World War, no doubt in Iraq as well, as the bombs rained down on Baghdad during Operation Shock and Awe. I saw a documentary where an Afghani woman was breastfeeding her baby in a cave in the early stages of the war with the Taliban. The women in desert tribes in

Africa used to tend to their livestock, give birth under a tree, cut the umbilical cord with a knife, and then return to the huts to feed their babies. Their husbands probably didn't even notice. If it could be done under such trying conditions why was it so difficult at the Mater Mothers' Hospital in Brisbane? Some women, the midwife told me as she helped Darlene, never managed to breastfeed and moved their babies straight on to the bottle and formula, which presented a whole new range of other problems, and I suspect was perhaps one reason behind high infant mortality rates in undeveloped countries and olden times.

Germaine Greer once said that women are good at guilt. As I was to learn over the next few months, breastfeeding was a perfect forum for them to display this trait, either about themselves, which they did brutally, or about others, which they did discreetly.

'But we must not give up so easily,' the midwife said sternly to Darlene as her spirits waned and the frustration crept in. 'There's nothing better than breastmilk.' I also recalled what my mother had said to me in the weeks leading up to the birth: 'Nobody thought anything of bottle-feeding your baby until the breastfeeding Nazis came along.' Then she rattled off some of the names of family friends, all big strapping lads, one of whom had played A-grade Rugby Union in Brisbane, who had been bottle-fed. Another had been a neighbour who was school captain of a prestigious girls' grammar school. I thought Mum was trying to give me a hint.

'So was I a bottle-fed baby, Mum?' It was a question I'd never even thought about before. What difference did it make anyway? I'd turned out fine, hadn't I? Mum seemed quite taken aback.

'How could you say such a thing after all I went through? No, I breastfed you till you were six months old. But your younger brother, well, I was so tired . . . it was my fourth after all . . . and after a few weeks it all became too difficult. These days the breastfeeding Nazis would have made me keep at it to try and keep the milk flowing.' I thought about my younger brother, a barrister, highly intelligent . . . but then his legs were always a little on the skinny side.

Fergus is still clutching at Darlene and falling away, and she is getting angry at herself while I silently pray to God for success, even though I haven't been to Mass for what must be decades and have forgotten the last time I took confession. My list of committed sins would be a frightful length after such an absence, with all the drinking and fornicating, and all the swearing and lying. I'm not sure the few Hail Marys Father Sherman gave me to say on my knees at the pew as penance for my sins back at school would cut it now. But then I never told Father Sherman the truth, did I? Did anybody?

I should have told him about how I was looking at Playboy magazines and fantasising about having sex with the good Catholic girls from our sister school down the road, whom we had to dance with on Friday afternoons. In church Father

Sherman said that thinking 'it' was just as bad as doing 'it', which really troubled me. If that was true then I was on an express train straight to hell. Andy took things to a whole new level when he told us about his fantasy, where one of the female teachers had a dungeon hidden below her desk and she disciplined him down there when he misbehaved in class. Instead, I confessed to Father Sherman that I'd told a few lies and been disrespectful to my parents; kept it pretty general really, which we'd all learned to do, although I did admit to stealing a Mars bar from the milk bar near the train station, which had been causing me no end of guilt.

'God forgives you for your sins,' Father Sherman said. 'Say three Hail Marys and two Our Fathers. Go in peace.' Instead of saying those prayers over and over I'd kneel there in front of the altar and the sculpture of Jesus suffering on the cross and tell God the real truth, about the magazines and the girls from the Catholic school; have an open and honest conversation. It was because of this that I always felt we had a pretty cosy relationship.

Outside of office hours, back at home, I used to pray to God quite regularly too, lying in bed at night asking him to give me hair under my arms. Andy and Nick were sailing through puberty with deepening voices and shaving kits to cope with the ludicrous amounts of excess hair sprouting forth from their bodies. I figured the hair and its indication of maturity was the sole reason for their success with girls, and my lack thereof. Girls from not just one but several Catholic schools throughout the city were falling for their charms, not to mention the colleges frequented by the Anglicans, Presbyterians and Lutherans. The language of love for them crossed all religious divides. Nick was still a virgin but he'd been given a head job by one of the female staff at McDonald's, where he worked on weekends and school holidays. That pretty much confirmed his status in the schoolyard as a legendary ladies' man. It must have been hard for God to decide who to help: the Ethiopians, dying of thirst and starvation, who Band Aid and Bob Geldof were trying to raise money for to feed the world, or me in suburban Brisbane, suffering from a lack of hair under my arms.

Once as I was lining up a difficult penalty in an important rugby game I started praying to God for strength because my legs were trembling from the nerves. More than anything I was worried about what my father would do to me if I missed it. The ball sailed neatly through the posts. As I ran back into position the crowd cheered and it was as though God was looking down on me, watching the game through the clouds gathering on the horizon because at that moment the sun sneaked through the gloom and started to shine. He must have been watching a kid from the other team, too, as he sliced through our defence and scored under the posts to beat us when victory seemed assured.

When I asked the Christian Brothers or the nuns about war and famine and why God let those things happen, why he let the brother of a friend at school drown in the swimming pool, why a neighbour had leukaemia and was going to die, they'd say that the Lord works in mysterious ways.

'Faith,' they said. 'You have to have faith.' One nun confused things even more by preaching to us that our creator was, in fact, a woman.

These days I'm the worst kind of Christian, the lukewarm variety who abstains from church and confession and prays only when I want something in return, never giving, just wanting to receive. But my cosy relationship with God seems to have evaporated as I'm not sure if he's up there listening anymore, especially outside office hours. According to the Bible, there is a special place in hell for fence sitters like me, the people who hedge their bets just in case, which makes me wonder why I even bother praying when it's only making things worse in the long run. But I will pray for my son. *Please, Lord, let him feed, please.*

When Fergus finally latched on it was as relieving as a soothing balm; as I was to discover, there is nothing quite so blissful as watching your child eat healthy food. You realise that you're just like every parent, like your own parents, even a bully like my dad, who went to church every Sunday for most of his life. We all want our kids to grow up big and strong. When Darlene's mum visited us in hospital I asked her how she coped when her kids were born. Nanna and Grampi, as we named them when Fergus was born, were originally from Adelaide. They were part of the migration to Queensland from the southern states in the late seventies and eighties.

'Everybody in those days read Dr Spock,' Nanna said. I was confused for a second, thinking of Leonard Nimoy from *Star*

Trek and Captain Kirk sitting in his seat on the *Enterprise* – what the hell has that to do with child rearing?

'Some of my friends swore by Dr Spock but Scott never responded to anything in the book.' She meant Uncle Scott, Darlene's brother, not the character Scotty of 'beam me up' fame. Uncle Scott was legendary in the family for his spectacular escapades when he was a toddler. They once found him on the roof of a building in an industrial estate in Woodside, hundreds of metres from their home, and they never worked out how the hell he got up there.

There seemed so much to worry about and it had only just begun. When we took Fergus out of hospital I couldn't believe we were being left in charge of a human being. The authorities are so entwined in our lives that we baulked for a second at the door to the lift: *Shouldn't we be signing a form, asking for permission to leave?* But they just let us walk away. Worse still for us, there would be no midwives to call when Fergus started crying. We weren't the only first-time parents relying on them. You'd hear the emergency buttons being pressed throughout the night, alarms going off and feet running down the hallways outside as the midwives dashed from one room to the next. They were like magicians, conjuring up silence amid the mayhem by using simple confidence tricks that we had yet to master. Sometimes it was as easy as adjusting the swaddling. How did they know from the cries of our child that he was cold?

We got so used to the midwives over the week we were at hospital that I couldn't imagine how we would cope without them. Would our baby freeze to death once he was left in the care of his clueless parents? Sending him home with us, complete amateurs, was like sending a primary school student out onto Lang Park to take the first hit up in a State of Origin.

I would also miss the morning breakfast trolley, when other dads would also emerge like zombies from stints on the recliner chairs in their rooms and start piling cereal, milk and toast or bacon and eggs onto trays for their hungry partners to consume in private behind closed doors. It didn't matter how many kids we'd sired, all of us had the dishevelled look of a man who knew he had moved one peg down the pecking order. Back home, as Darlene and I struggled to find the time to feed ourselves, the breakfast trolley seemed like a long-since-forgotten pleasant dream. I would have paid hundreds to that nice old lady who pushed it if she would just knock on our door every morning and take the pressure off us preparing meals during those difficult first six months.

Down in the car park I had loaded Fergus into the back of my dark blue Ford Laser hatchback, which up until now had served its purpose – running me about town, room in the boot for my surfboard or golf clubs or the groceries with the back seat always folded down. But now the car seemed too low and too small and dangerously unsafe for the purpose of carrying a child. With the back seat up how were we going to fit a pram inside? Grampi had already pointed out that there were no airbags or anti-lock brakes. I promised myself I would find the money to buy the biggest, ugliest four-wheel drive on the market, maybe one of those Hummers that rap stars drive in the States, something with steel-plated armour that not even a missile could penetrate and cause harm to my child. I now understood why so many mums own four-wheel drives. It didn't matter that they roll like drums if they are in an accident. There is a supreme feeling of safety being up high and in control of something powerful.

Darlene, still in pain from the operation and with a worried expression on her face, watched anxiously as I fumbled with the straps on the newly purchased and bulky baby capsule. I was terrified that Fergus would break in half as I buckled him in. I moved with the slow, controlled movements of someone placing a glass vase inside a box for the removalist's van. If there'd been styrofoam packing chips or scrunched up pieces of newspaper I would have used them, scattering them about the empty spaces between Fergus's arms and legs. I didn't know then that fragility in babies is just an illusion – they are designed to withstand all manner of bumps and scrapes. Andy said he was just the same with their first but by the third he just chucked his son on the back seat much like a football.

I drove home so slowly from the Mater Mothers' Hospital that people behind us were honking their horns. Even Darlene thought I was taking things a bit too cautiously.

'What are we in, *Driving Miss Daisy*?'

We went straight to a Christmas lunch at my sister's place at Toowong and Fergus was handed around like the present that he certainly was. Darlene had bought a red Santa's hat for him and he looked like one of Santa's elves as his cousins took their turns holding him in their laps under the Christmas tree while he slept. I never tired of holding him, of stretching out his long arms and legs, of putting my hand on his chest and feeling his heart beat. I liked taking off my shirt and laying him on my chest, cherishing the skin-to-skin contact, and the wonderful baby smell of him.

He'd been average weight but quite long for a newborn. The nurse who measured him looked at me, a few inches over six feet, and said, 'Well, that makes sense.' Every time someone we knew looked at him they'd give their judgment about whom he took after. The verdict seemed split down the middle. *Oh he looks gorgeous, just like his mother. Oh he's handsome, just like his father*, which I always found amusing because they would never say he's ugly, just like his father. Or the occasional, *geez, he looks nothing like either of you*. I made a mental note to tell the next parent I met how much their baby looked like both of them because as a parent that's all you want to hear, that's the diplomatic approach that works best. No one wants to hear the truth.

When we took him out to a café on Boxing Day I would never have guessed how much a baby connects you to the community. A young woman came over and said to Darlene, 'I just want you to know how beautiful your baby is.' Everywhere we took him people would be smiling. Old ladies especially loved coming up and asking questions.

'And how old is this little one?' As Fergus grew older I started getting confused about the months you have to use to answer the age question . . . was he three months old or four months? But then I was never very good with numbers and the lack of sleep was playing havoc with my brain. I wondered about when it would end. When Fergus is a twenty-year-old would I be saying my son is two hundred and forty months? On the positive side, though, who would have thought that having a baby would elicit such a response from complete strangers and bring so much happiness? The presence of a baby is the ultimate icebreaker. You could have a conversation with anyone. Of course, this was before the colic arrived. It didn't take me long to work out that colic is a fancy medical term for the fact that the doctors don't have a clue what's wrong. With his red face, booming voice and reflux there weren't as many people smiling or keen to come up and have a chat.

Despite the attention, we learned quickly that newborns were still frowned upon at some places. At a popular bookstore in the inner suburbs we positively cleared their café upon arrival as several sets of eyes went from Darlene to the baby and to me with my pram packed with essentials, as if we were going on a three-day hiking adventure. I was getting used to the smiles so the frosty reception came as quite a surprise. When Darlene began breastfeeding discreetly with a wrap over her shoulder to cover her nakedness one of the waiters could barely hide his annoyance. Fergus never made a sound. When I told my mother she said, 'Well, what do you expect? In my day we had to hide at home. We would never have dreamed of going out to a bookstore.' At another café in the city the manager made it known that perhaps we'd be more comfortable somewhere else and I followed her into the kitchen and let her have a piece of my mind about discrimination.

★

For the first few months after Fergus came home it seemed as if every second of the day I was standing by the washing machine, then hanging out the baby clothes, towels and blankets that had piled up in the laundry basket with astonishing speed. Fergus was a spewer, constantly regurgitating over our clothes when we held him, or on the rug when we placed him on the ground, just like his mother, apparently.

'Darlene was forever throwing up on me,' Nanna had said when she came to visit one weekend. She had said it so fondly, like she was reliving a pleasant memory, although it occurred to me that we have an amazing ability to sugar-coat the past and make it seem like everything is fantastic. My grandad used to talk about the good old days and I believed him until I realised he'd lived through two world wars, when millions of people were killed – basically the most violent era in human history. But to Grandad people left their doors open and everyone was much friendlier than they are today. I'm sure at the time Nanna would have been just as anxious about all the work Darlene's constant vomiting required as we were now with Fergus. I looked at my mother-in-law and then at my beautiful wife, on her knees happily arranging a series of spew cloths about our son's head in preparation for the liquid landslide, and wondered about the strange powers of genetics.

As I later hung out the washing on the line at the side of the house I thought about a single mother I used to work with. How had she managed to return to work after just a few weeks? People warn you about sleep deprivation and all the work a baby involves, and you read all the literature you can on the subject, but until you experience it for yourself you never really know the monumental shift a baby brings into your life. That girl I worked with always looked so desperately tired. Looking back, it didn't seem possible that she could have done all this washing and breastfeeding and still got to work on time in the morning, which she didn't a lot of the time much to the chagrin of the chief of staff. Like the curtain being lifted on the first act of a drama, I now understood. I felt like ringing her up and telling her what a prick the boss had been.

Not long after we brought Fergus home from hospital I wondered when the worrying might stop. I asked my sister for advice. She went to her television cabinet and tossed me a DVD of the movie *Parenthood*. She said the answer I sought would be found there. She was right. There's a scene where Steve Martin's dad explains that the worrying never ends when you're a parent: 'You never cross the goal line, spike the ball and do your touchdown dance, never.' It was beautifully done but it didn't make me feel any better. The worrying that something awful might happen started before Fergus was born and had slowly escalated month after month. When you start worrying about the worrying you know you're in trouble.

When I asked Sally if she worried about her kids she gave me her much-loved copy of *Buddhism for Mothers*. The theory was, if I meditated and smiled a lot and accepted that there is pain and suffering in the world then I would be better for it. I didn't want to think about pain and suffering in the world, which all sounded a little pessimistic, and when was I ever going to get the time to meditate? We were so terrified that Fergus might stop breathing we even made the mistake other first-time parents probably make and let him sleep in our room. Darlene had done all this work on the nursery, which looked like something out of *House & Garden*, but we were too afraid to use it. I would wake up and check his swaddling, that he wasn't too hot or too cold, making sure he was always on his back.

One day while cuddling him in front of the television my fingers stumbled upon the imperfection forming across the back of his head. I ran my fingers over it again and again. *Holy shit, what the fuck is happening here!* It was all I could do to stop myself from picking up the mobile and ringing triple zero. The back of his head had started going flat, like the bottom of a frying pan. The doctor said the flat head was from sleeping on his back and nothing to worry about. He reassured us that babies' heads are soft and malleable and it would go away over time but I still worried that he'd be teased at school for having a pan head and that it would be my fault. Perhaps he would pick up a nickname like one of my childhood Rugby League heroes from the Norths Devils: Dishhead Dowling. If I was overly concerned, the doctor said, we could buy a helmet that would help mould his head back into shape. I looked these helmets up on the internet and saw babies who looked like Evel Knievel, the daredevil who tried to jump over all those buses at Wembley Stadium years ago but only managed to break just about every bone in his body in the process. After the *Six Million Dollar Man*, Evel Knievel was about the coolest person in the world when I was a kid, but there was no way I wanted my son wearing one of those helmets. I was overly concerned but not quite at the helmet-wearing stage yet.

As a sort of counterbalance to the flat head I'd sometimes ignore the experts' advice and lay him on his stomach with his head to the side during afternoon sleeps, and watch him like a hawk. When I wasn't worrying about flat-head syndrome I worried myself sick about sudden infant death syndrome; whether Fergus would be breathing when I checked on him in the morning, or lying stiff and cold in his bassinet. I re-read the chapter in *Buddhism for Mothers* called 'Worrying about Our Children'. I resigned myself to the fact that if it was going to happen then it was going to happen, it was in God's hands — even though the Buddhists don't believe in God — and there was absolutely nothing I could do about it. This gave me a certain peace of mind, and thankfully it never happened. I'd read stories in the newspapers about those who had suffered the loss of their child and I walked around for a while thinking about how they could have even coped with the grief. One mother who'd lost her child to SIDS said people told her how much they admired her strength because 'if the same thing happened to me I wouldn't be able to cope'.

'Well, what choice do I have?' she said. 'All I've got left to do is cope.'

Fergus would sleep for an hour or two at a time and even though there were two of us to cater for his every whim both of us were soon exhausted. Of an evening we'd put him to bed at 7pm and Darlene would get up again for his night-time feed at 10pm. At midnight he'd be up again, then at 2am, then 4am . . . For Darlene it was worse as she was breastfeeding, which meant, to a certain extent, I was off the hook.

Sally was not impressed with this arrangement because Andy had helped her feed their babies. She had expressed her milk into bottles, which he then got out of the fridge and reheated in the middle of the night while she slept. At the time he had complained to me in a sad tired voice while rubbing his bloodshot eyes that the late-night feeds were slowly killing him. I'd told Andy he had to stand up to his wife as he had to work the next day; she was the primary carer and had to shoulder the burden. I am secretly scared of Andy's wife, as I'm sure Andy is too.

Apart from her nipple guards Sally also gave Darlene her breast pump, saying, 'This will make sure he pulls his weight.' Darlene hated the squeaking noise it made, though, and the feeling that she was being pumped up like a football. She gave up after hours of bicep-bulging work, to be rewarded with just a few milky drops. We ordered an automatic machine from the Australian Breastfeeding Association, which I picked up from a lady at Kenmore. She wasn't wearing a bra and her boobs hung down to her waist. I selfishly wondered what the sucking and pulling from something that looked like an early IBM computer would do to my wife's figure. There was no squeaking from the contraption but being hooked up to a machine made Darlene feel like she was a dairy cow getting milked at the farm. It didn't work for her either. Then the mastitis hit and more often than not I would be woken anyway during the night to massage away the blockages.

I was about to become a stay-at-home dad, so I thought I was at one with my fellow sisters-in-arms, having travelled through all the mastitis and breastfeeding trials. I was even hoping Sally might invite me to join her mothers' group. But at a dinner party a few months later the women present turned on me when I mentioned that I wanted Darlene to breast-feed for as long as possible because 'there's nothing better than breastmilk'.

'Oh, that's big of you,' Nick's girlfriend at the time said. Then I thought about the nipple guards as she spat out, 'I'd like to see you with your tits out getting sucked dry every day and night.' Sally just glared at me.

3

DOUBLE, DOUBLE TOIL AND TROUBLE

The excitement and adrenalin of the birth sustained me for
the first few weeks after Fergus's arrival home. I just sat there
with him on my lap, staring at him, playing with his hands
and fingers, captivated by his beautiful peaceful face, his long
perfect limbs. I'd lay him on my chest, breathing in his wonderful baby smell. But soon the tiredness took over and with
it more complicated emotions pushed their way to the surface.
If I was in love with my son, which I clearly was, why then
was I becoming increasingly angry at the world?

I developed a strange habit of occasionally chanting under
my breath the scene from Shakespeare's *Macbeth*, which I'd

studied at school, where the three witches are standing around a boiling cauldron: *Double, double toil and trouble; Fire burn, and cauldron bubble.* I had played the part of one of the witches in the class production, which hadn't gone well because Nick, dressed as Macbeth, flashed a browneye at me from stage right. My English and Drama teacher, who couldn't see Nick, didn't appreciate me breaking character. Nick, of course, got full marks, appearing onstage without distractions in his black tights full of confidence: *How now, you secret, black, and midnight hags?*

When I was driving the car without the baby it was all I could do to not run those who dawdled below the speed limit off the road. People irritated me. Personalised numberplates irritated me. 'GR8 DAY'! Or what they thought were amusing stickers on their car: 'My other car is a Mercedes-Benz' or 'Fartaholic on board'. Why did they feel the need to share with the world any problems they had with status or their smelly bottom? When I dashed into Coles to pick up some nappies I'd be counting the number of items in people's baskets in the express lane, wanting to throttle them if they had so much as a margarine tub too many.

Could I blame all this anger on tiredness? Maybe, but there was something deeper going on, at the inner core of me, something I didn't want to acknowledge. Perhaps I was like my father after all. When I thought about him my heart started thumping in my chest.

★

Not long after the birth we headed to the Gold Coast for a family holiday at Greenmount. The unit had been paid a year in advance by Nanna and Grampi, before Darlene was even pregnant, and we did not want to let our new addition dictate our lives.

'So what if we have a newborn,' Darlene said. 'It doesn't mean we can't still enjoy the beach.'

Try as everybody might, a newborn and a two-bedroom unit don't leave much space for privacy, especially when you're dossing on a fold-out sofa bed and sharing a bathroom with Fergus's doting great-grandmother aged in her eighties. Further complicating matters was that Grampi had taken to wearing around the unit with great pride the kilt we'd given him for his sixtieth birthday. All that separated us from whatever he wore underneath was the bluish-grey tartan favoured by the Clark clan. My joke that Duncan the Fat, ancestor of the Robertsons, used to eat the Clarks with his haggis was also wearing a bit thin.

At night Nanna and Grampi would put on oxygen masks and attach themselves to bulky machines that helped with their sleep apnoea. A few days into the holiday I slipped out of the building at about five o'clock one morning, hoping that the benefits of a walk might help invigorate my senses and remove the rage eating away at me. I closed the door while Darlene and Fergus were contentedly dozing and Nanna and Grampi were sprawled on their king-sized bed, doing their best Darth Vader impersonations attached to their his-and-hers ResMed machines.

I trudged around the headland at Kirra, sucking in the fresh sea air, mingling with other walkers and joggers. It was a pristine morning, the sun sitting just above the waterline on the horizon, slowly climbing into the sky. Out on the ocean surfers were already making the most of the glassy conditions courtesy of a light offshore breeze. The endorphins from the exercise started to improve my mood. U2's 'Beautiful Day' had replaced the inner chant of *double, double toil and trouble*. Not far from home after an hour on the track I passed a young man in board shorts and thongs. He was enjoying the early morning sunshine on his back as he strolled along in no particular hurry. There was the faint whiff of stale alcohol about him and it occurred to me that he might be heading home after a big night out. I heard him mumble something.

'You say something?' I asked.

'Your shirt's on inside out, dude,' he replied.

I stopped, looked down and sure enough he was correct. My high-rise unit was looming in the distance; there were only a few hundred metres till I got to the safety of home.

'Ah, what can you do?' I said, trying to sound philosophical.

'Well, you could take it off and put it round the right way,' he replied, actually sounding like a philosopher. Perhaps it was the condescending tone or the cheeky grin as he said it but a red mist descended on me. I thought about hitting him. I really did. I was staring at his Adam's apple, imagining him withering on the walking track after I'd karate-chopped it through the back of his neck. He sensed the anger as I came at him. He was looking at my clenched fists.

'Hey, relax, dude,' the young man said. 'I'm just trying to help.' His back was to a wooden fence against the sand dunes. He was cornered as we stood facing each other.

'You're not worth it,' I said, turning around.

'It's okay to be embarrassed, fella,' he shouted at me as I marched off. 'We all make mistakes you know. Have a nice day, you grumpy prick.'

When I told Darlene and her parents about the psycho I had run into on the walking track they looked at each other as if they were in on a secret that had so far eluded me. Darlene was breastfeeding Fergus. Nanna and Grampi were eating muesli at the table.

'I think we all know who the psycho is,' Fergus's great-grandmother shouted from the balcony as she sipped her morning cuppa.

Not long after our holiday Darlene got a letter in the mail, which caused us much excitement. Before Fergus's birth we had entered a competition to take part in a pictorial coffee-table book about the babies of Brisbane. The $50 application fee would be donated to the Royal Brisbane and Women's Hospital. If selected, we got our photo taken for the book and the opportunity to maybe purchase some of the pictures taken by the photographer. No obligation. It seemed like a pretty good deal. And – surprise, surprise – we were selected.

We were told to dress in black T-shirts and a few days later we arrived at the studio in suburban Graceville, where a photographer was perched on a stepladder surrounded by lots of bright lights stuck inside umbrellas. She took photos of us holding Fergus, who was stark naked, while we kissed and cuddled him in various poses – cradled in our forearms, peeking over our shoulders, being smooched lovingly on his forehead. The fact he was sans clothes seemed a dangerous manoeuvre. My fears were well justified when a golden twinkle arched through the air much like a cherub in a fountain, soiling in crisscross strokes the designer T-shirt from Industrie that Darlene had paid a small fortune for from a boutique in the Valley. Turns out, the urine was the least of our worries, a mere entrée to the smorgasbord of bodily fluids and excrements that exploded from his tiny body.

'Abandon ship! It's coming out of every orifice,' the photographer cried out towards the end of the shoot.

A few weeks later the owner of the photography studio ushered us into a darkened room where a comfy couch was positioned in front of a wide projection screen. He had a trendy David Beckham haircut in the mini–Mohawk style and his pointy shoes poking out from the bottom of his stonewashed jeans were made of the finest leather. We were each given coffees made from an Italian-designed stainless steel machine.

'Remember you don't have to buy anything, you're under no obligation,' he said as he presses a button and Robbie Williams' 'Angels' starts playing. Soon a series of gorgeous shots came up one after the other, a magnificent collage of breathtaking images miraculously taken between the various bombardments. How had the photographer managed this miracle? Tears rolled down Darlene's face. Her mother was dabbing at her eyes with a hanky.

'Shit,' I think as I sip my cappuccino, 'we'll have to buy them all. We're up for bloody thousands.'

A few weeks later Andy invited me on a camping trip. Andy and Sally have three children under five and they knew the importance of rest.

'We know what you and Darlene are going through,' Sally said. 'You can't possibly understand how tiring a baby is until you've been through it yourself.' Andy had also heard the story about the man who told me to turn my shirt around the right way. He suggested a few nights at Inskip Point near Rainbow Beach might be just the remedy for a tired father in need of sleep.

'We'll fish for whiting and flathead. You'll have your own tent,' Andy said. 'You'll come back a better dad and a better husband.'

Darlene seemed happy enough to let me go. In fact, she almost pushed me out the door. Nanna too seemed pleased for the chance to come over and help look after her new grandson and spend some bonding time with her daughter. We arrived at the point on a Thursday morning and secured an idyllic spot within the banksia woodlands with views of the wide headland beach and Fraser Island. Summer was drawing to a close. The air smelled warm, sweet and dry like the gum trees and salty like the ocean. Andy had a small fast runabout and we laid crab pots in Tin Can Bay – 'I love the smell of four-stroke in the morning,' he said as he revved the Yamaha motor – returning to the campfire to drink beer and nips of Bundaberg Rum while Andy cooked our dinner over a portable gas grill. The only hitch to our perfect day was that, due to the absence of any nibbles, we had to purchase our whiting fillets from the fish shop in town.

We talked about Nick for a while. He was prone these days to complaining about how boring we'd all become. While the arrival of a baby in my life had been greeted joyously I couldn't help but detect a certain sadness about Nick, like he knew a part of his life had died with the birth of new life in mine. My new commitments seemed to counterbalance Nick's spectacular single life of non-commitments. He goes travelling with his girlfriends to exotic locales, hiking in Nepal, skiing in Colorado, and surfing in Indonesia; talks about movies and restaurants that Andy and I will never get to see unless we hire a babysitter. Shit, he lived in a different stratosphere and still goes to nightclubs and dance parties, drops Es and snorts the odd line of cocaine when the mood takes him.

'That bastard still has sex several times a week,' Andy said, staring into the fire. After a while Andy told me, 'You know I admire you for what you're going to do. Being a stay-at-home dad. I'd go mad if I was stuck in the house with the kids. The only place where I can get any peace and quiet when I'm home from work is in the toilet. Sometimes I stay in there so long reading the newspaper that my legs go to sleep and I have trouble standing up. Eventually they find me. Sometimes it only takes seconds. They smash on the door, bang, bang, bang, and demand to know what I'm doing. "Come out,

Daddy. Come out." I'm trying to read the sports pages and they pound on that door like Jack Nicolson in *The Shining*.'

Eventually, like it always does, the conversation turned to funny stories from school and how much life had changed. At Schoolies Week in the eighties the old Broadbeach Hotel on the Gold Coast welcomed Andy, Nick and me with jugs of warm frothy lager until the steroid-ridden bouncers, appalled at our condition, hurled us out of the beer garden towards the sand dunes. There'd been rugby tours down south, bucks parties, fishing trips on Moreton Bay and B&S balls out west at places with wild names like Nindigully. Andy and I once jumped the fence at the US Masters golf tournament on the Sunday morning and hid in the bushes until the final round started. We discussed what would have happened if the police had caught us. This was the town of Augusta in the Deep South. Trespassers are frowned upon. Perhaps we would have been beaten with batons or even shot by the guards. But they didn't catch us did they? We walked out the front gates in the twilight singing 'Georgia on My Mind', both of us with cuts from the barbed-wire fence, declaring it to be the single greatest achievement of our lives to date. Marriage and children a decade later would see it move down the list.

We liked talking about our adventures because it reminded us of a time when we were brave and foolhardy, prepared to take on anything. We'd canoed down the Zambezi River in Africa dodging hippos, elephants and crocodiles. We'd all tried our luck in London on work visas, travelling through Europe when we had enough money. Nick took me to Amsterdam and helped me negotiate the cold tram-filled and bike-filled streets to the backpackers in the red-light district when I freaked out in Madame Tussauds – I thought one hash cookie would be enough but it had been so tasty I ate two. It was Boris Becker who tipped me over the edge, standing there with his tennis racquet beside Harrison Ford dressed as Indiana Jones. Their cold lifeless wax skins seem to sweat under the bright lights and I thought I saw them move. In Marrakech we marvelled at the snake charmers, jugglers and fortune tellers. Nick got food poisoning after insisting on eating Moroccan delicacies cooked at a stall run by no other than Muhammad Ali. Ali's food had the punching power of his namesake, and when Nick's stomach swelled up afterwards like he'd swallowed a watermelon, I was the one who had to look after him.

After a few hours of reminiscing I asked Andy, 'Why didn't you tell me camping was so relaxing?'

'The thing with camping,' Andy replied, turning serious, 'is that it can be awesome one moment then really bad the next. Much like children, it teaches you to live in the moment.' When Andy talked about camping and children he sounded like the author of *Buddhism for Mothers*.

The next day things turned bad. Really quickly. The sky grew dark and a light drizzle started falling. Again we caught no fish. The crab pots we'd laid overnight had been stolen.

'Who steals a man's crab pots?' Andy lamented into the stormy sky from the bow of his runabout, sounding like the ancient mariner. 'It violates the unwritten law of the ocean.' Then, when we returned to the campsite a gang of rough types had parked their trailer within several inches of my tiny one-man tent. Their leader had long black greasy hair and a glass eye. He was drinking from a stubby of VB as a gaggle of unwashed children and three unleashed dogs scurried about his legs. He did not look like the kind of person with whom you negotiate. Besides, I did not know the rules of camping and whether it was poor form to camp so close to someone else's spot.

'It's an old camping trick,' Andy seethed. 'They are jealous of our magnificent position so they are going to camp us out.'

'Camp us out?'

'Weight in numbers. There's hundreds of the bastards. We're screwed.'

As the sun set they started on the bourbon and colas, pre-mixed in a can. The music got louder. One of them had a guitar and played it very badly. At midnight it was like I had pitched my tent on Brunswick Street in Fortitude Valley. I lay there in my sleeping bag and boiled with rage, cursing my luck and my tremendous tiredness, but it wasn't until I heard one of them say that they should stay up and watch the sun come up that I lost it. I let the anger embrace me. It picked me up and swept me to the edge of their campfire. The sound of the surf nearby was surging in my ears.

'I have a newborn,' I screamed. 'I came here to get some fucking rest!'

We listened to sad Johnny Cash songs all the way home to Brisbane in Andy's grey Prado.

4

REVERSING OUT

Darlene is crying in the garage. She does not want to go back to work.

'I feel guilty,' she says. 'I'm abandoning my baby.' Then she puts her head on the steering wheel of her car and it's almost as if she's drowning because every few seconds she comes up for air to catch her breath. I'm still in my blue-and-white striped Country Road pyjamas and matching slippers that Darlene bought me for my birthday, bed hair sticking out in clumps, rocking Fergus back and forth in my arms, hoping that the scene playing out before him won't become lodged somewhere in his subconscious. I reach through the open driver's side window and stroke her cheek but the gesture seems woefully inadequate. *Shit, where had this come from?*

There had been no warning signs of a meltdown last night. If I remembered correctly Darlene had been quite enthusiastic about returning to the office. She loved her job. How stupid and insensitive I must be not to have seen that her upbeat mood was a smokescreen for the torture going on inside. I thought again about Germaine Greer and the guilt. Unfortunately it wouldn't be the first time I'd see the awful toll guilt takes on mothers who work.

On paper, everything made perfect sense before Fergus was born. Darlene would go back to her work as a project director after maternity leave. She had spent over ten years climbing the corporate ladder, competing against men in the very male-dominated world of property development. For all the testosterone in her industry, her employer, a large multinational with offices around the world, was way ahead of most businesses in Australia when it came to maternity leave, offering generous paid leave for its female employees and even some time off for dads. Darlene had some holiday time owing, too, which was tacked onto her package. Six months seemed like more than enough time for us to adjust to our new life with a baby. In fact six months seemed like heaven when the most we'd ever spent together without working was a lousy two weeks each year, usually over Christmas.

The property industry pays quite well. Darlene earned much more money than I did. Much more. It wasn't even a contest. I had never planned on being a stay-at-home dad, although adjusting to life on my wage alone clearly did not make economic sense. I needed a break from my job in the media anyway – unpredictable hours, ethical and moral dilemmas waiting to mug me around every corner, quandaries that haunt me still. Where is the enjoyment in knocking on doors when loved ones had been killed in shark attacks? *How do you feel?* Or in seeing dead people mangled up in car accidents, a crushed motorcyclist's legs sticking out from under the wheel of a semi-trailer. *Who, What, When, Where, Why and How.*

Once I interviewed a homicide detective next to a huge pool of black congealed blood that smelled sickly sweet in the humidity and was thick with fat green blowflies. The body had lain for days in the house in the Queensland heat before they took it away. The cop was old school, casually chewing on some gum, as he gave me the details. They were looking for a car seen driving away from the house around the time of the murder. I'm pretty sure he was trying to freak me out, which he did. On the way back to the newsroom I worried that the stench was stuck in my nostrils and I'd never be able to wash it out. And then there is the image of a baby lying dead on the footpath in suburban Brisbane – shot through the head by its father with a .22 rifle – that still haunts me, the little white sheet that looked more like a large napkin being pulled back by police as a female relative shrieks. Yes, being a stay-at-home dad was a much better option than going back to the perils of work at a newspaper or television station. How hard can it be after all, looking after a baby?

The challenge of it appealed to me. Role reversal was still uncommon and I would be a rare species, although from what I'd read more and more fathers were taking up the challenge. Sure, I'd have to endure some difficult moments. Maybe take a hit to my ego. But other, braver men had already paved the way and taken some of the hits for me. They talked about being ignored by mothers at playgrounds and parks. They told you how doctors always talk to the mother, even when both parents are present. It was always assumed dad works and mum stays at home to look after the kids. But society was now slowly becoming less judgmental, more understanding, especially since John Lennon led the way, staying at home for five years with Sean. The movies caught on with Michael Keaton showing how it was done in *Mr Mom*. Momentum had been building for two decades before I came along. Even *60 Minutes* did a story on stay-at-home dads. Plus I had a burning desire to be a super dad, to prove that I could do a better job than *he* ever could. It would only be for a little while anyway, until we worked things out. Everything would be fine.

We'd been together for six years before we married, the delay due mainly to my commitment issues. When you've grown up with parents who sleep in separate rooms at opposite ends of the house and meet every night to fight at the dinner table you'd be forgiven for thinking that marriage doesn't seem like the most appealing option. After the wedding, a year passed before Darlene fell pregnant. Along the way there had been the heartache of a miscarriage. A young doctor at the Wesley Hospital had congratulated us on being pregnant for us to lose the baby only 24 hours later. Turned out it was an ectopic pregnancy – the foetus developing outside the uterus in the fallopian tube and never having a chance – which didn't help numb the pain of our loss. Darlene bled so much from the miscarriage she fainted on the floor of the bathroom in Sydney, almost breaking her nose and knocking out one of her front teeth. She missed the wedding of her good friend later that day as we spent it in the emergency room at the Royal Prince Alfred Hospital. They examined her carefully and did some tests and X-rays before calling in a dentist to work on her tooth. I squeezed her hand so tightly she complained it hurt more than the huge needle that was stuck into her gums. Afterwards they took her away to another room and asked her in hushed tones, now that she was alone, whether I had bashed her up. *Did you really faint and fall over?* I understand why they have to ask such things but I'm glad she told me they did so after we'd gotten home.

We were disturbed for months by the awkwardness and, in a weird kind of way, by the shame of the miscarriage. We were hiding at home, not going out. It was an experience we suffered behind our wall of silence but decided that per-haps it would be better if we opened up to our family and friends about what was bothering us. What was the point of holding all that misery inside anyway when it would probably only manifest itself in other ways? What were we hiding from anyway? When told, Darlene's grandmother revealed a pain-ful family secret: she had endured several miscarriages before Darlene's mother was born.

'I kept that to myself for many years,' she said. Sally too had had a miscarriage – and I thought I knew everything that was going on in their lives.

'We always regretted not telling people,' Andy said. I thought I was a good friend to Andy. How had I missed it? Nick too was very understanding and I was surprised at how tragedy cements the bonds of friendship, which isn't always about celebrations and good times and flashing browneyes as you act in *Macbeth*.

Over the next few weeks I lay awake at night wondering if I'd ever get a chance to be a father. What sort of father would I make anyway? I didn't exactly have the greatest template from which to draw inspiration. To me, being a father meant coming home from work, brooding in a cave, screaming at the kids for ruining my marriage, seeing my partner recoil in horror when I touched her. Maybe it would be better for all involved if I was never a father to anyone.

My doubts about fatherhood were soothed by the knowledge that Darlene would make a terrific mother. We liked going for long walks after work with our dog and we'd pass kids playing on the swings and jungle gyms in the park. I could see her staring wistfully at other people's children in shops and cafés. It would be a tragedy if motherhood was denied to her. I knew what she was thinking. *What if I never get another chance?* I was a hypocrite again and prayed to God, knowing that Darlene would never resort to such ridiculousness. And then Darlene got pregnant – and stayed pregnant.

Up until this point in our relationship our combined wages had yielded powerful results. We'd scraped and saved to buy

a two-bedroomed worker's cottage in the leafy western suburbs of Brisbane, a short drive from the historic Walter Taylor
Bridge that spans the twisting serpentine reaches of the river.
Luckily, we bought the house before the property boom that
started around the time the Twin Towers came tumbling
down, but in truth there was very little luck about it. Darlene, with her expertise on such matters, had seen the signs
well before most. Sometimes I wonder how different our lives
would have been if we hadn't got in when we did, for within
the space of a few months prices started rocketing out of control, leaving many potential first-home buyers in their wake.
About the same time I'd started reading books about the stock
market, beginning a modest share portfolio that I controlled
through an online broking account. We were what demog-
raphers call DINKS – double income no kids – an emerging
phenomenon across the country at the time.

Thanks to feminists like Germaine Greer and Brisbane
local Merle Thornton, who is the mother of actress Sigrid
Thornton, women had taken control of their lives, careers
and destinies. In 1965, not long before I was born, Merle and
her friend Rosalie chained their ankles to a railing after being
refused a drink at the Regatta Hotel. Just down the road from
the Regatta at Wests Bulldogs on Sylvan Road at Toowong,
I remember playing football with the son of another trailblazer, Quentin Bryce, the Governor-General of Australia.
Back then, she was a law lecturer at the University of Queensland and later the Federal Sex Discrimination Commissioner.
I remember one of the fathers saying that she was 'bra burner'.

As a seven-year-old, I couldn't imagine her burning her bra or why she'd want to do such a thing, not knowing what it meant. She seemed so glamorous standing there on the sidelines. Now I know that women like Quentin Bryce paved the way for Darlene and, in a weird kind of way, for men like me, who would one day stay at home to look after the kids because their wives had stellar careers.

Courtesy of our combined purchasing power and the absence of children draining financial reserves, the opportunities for us at the time seemed boundless. Our little Queenslander and the share portfolio quickly doubled in value through no great brilliance on our part, although for a time I was under the illusion that I was blessed with a Gordon Gekko-like gift for share trading. I imagined lazing about the pool with a computer on my lap, trading shares and making my fortune. Everyone, it seemed, was making money in the noughties, renovating and trading up, which we did twice to great effect.

Why hadn't anyone told me about the stock market and how easy it was to make money before? A company I'd invested in was taken over by a larger rival and I was stunned at the huge profits that could be made in a day. You bought something, anything really: mining stocks with colourful names like Lynas Corporation and Paladin Energy; biotechs promising cures for cancer; investment banks like Macquarie, which they called the 'millionaires factory'; or, best of all, the income-producing real-estate investment trusts. Some financial planners were telling clients to borrow against their houses to further increase their wealth, organising huge margin loans as well as taking them on trips to Europe and treating them to fancy-dress balls where they dressed up as French aristocrats. And up and up the stock market skyrocketed, adding a lovely green tinge to the colour of my portfolio.

With so much information available on the internet it seemed easy to make educated decisions on which stocks might start to fire but then, looking back, it was almost impossible to pick a loser. Only the wise words of Andy, who worked in finance, urged caution. He used big phrases like 'subprime mortgage' and 'collatorised debt obligations'.

'Some hedge funds and contrary investors are going short on these,' he said and I had no idea what he was talking about. Once when we were playing golf he told me that Warren Buffett had said that 'nothing sedates rationality like large doses of easy money'. I Googled Warren Buffett when I got home. They called him the oracle of Omaha, the world's greatest investor. There were more aphorisms, all whimsical and profound: 'You only see who's swimming naked when the tide goes out.' He talked about market speculators being like Cinderella at the ball: 'But then it's midnight and everyone turns into pumpkins and mice.'

Still, with Darlene pregnant it didn't seem a stretch for me to quit my job and make extra income trading shares while looking after a baby as well. It took only a few minutes each day to check the portfolio and make some prudent decisions on what to buy and sell. Of course, Gordon Gekko wasn't a stay-at-home dad, was he? And I didn't know that a few minutes to yourself don't exist, let alone a few seconds when there is a newborn in the house. It was just like Andy had warned while camping; you're flat out going to the toilet let alone making prudent financial decisions. And the global financial crisis was waiting just around the corner.

The garage door of our rented house in Ipswich opens with a shudder and Darlene unwillingly reverses out. Living in Ipswich, a satellite city near Brisbane, might not sound to those in the know like a move to a better life, as Ipswich is sometimes seen as the ugly sibling to her glamorous big sister, but it was a calculated move on our part to save money for our next property purchase. For such a beautiful house in a child-friendly location the rent was ridiculously cheap, about half what you'd pay for a similar place in Brisbane. It was also closer to Darlene's work in the fledgling suburbs she was helping to build on the city fringes. Her company dug holes in the ground, filled them with water and built thriving communities around them. When they released land people were camping out to secure the best parcels.

Our rented house was on a prestigious golfing estate that had an impressive entrance with ponds and fig trees, manicured parks, playgrounds for the kids, and a course designed by the Great White Shark himself, golfing legend Greg Norman. Before I quit my job in the media to be a stay-at-home dad I'd interviewed 'The Shark' at the clubhouse and stood on the tee with him with a small group of journalists and sporting stars before we played some of the newly built holes. Allan Border, the former captain of the Australian cricket team, was there and seemed just as nervous as the rest of us, fidgeting and shuffling his feet. The Shark, when he arrived in a chauffeur-driven white Holden, was confident and larger than life. His tanned skin seemed to glow like he was a movie star. He had a firm grip when he shook my hand and his eyes, set back deep in his face, looked over us from behind a beaked nose, as if he was checking us out for weaknesses in our games, of which there were many.

He hit first and the ball exploded off his club, dissecting the fairway. Allan Border, a leftie, snuck one down the fairway with a lovely compact swing. One of the other journalists standing with me went next, walking to the tee almost like he was walking to the gallows, snap hooking his drive into a large ironbark off the fairway, where it bounced back down the cart path almost to Greg Norman's shiny golf spikes.

'I could always cut that tree down for you, mate,' The Shark said, and everyone fell about laughing. My shot, as I stood trembling on the tee, was not much better, and I was hoping The Shark might say something witty too so I could tell Andy and Nick. He just stood there, silent and unimpressed, eyes blazing, with his arms folded across his chest. After we played golf I asked him if he ever went to the Brekkie Creek for a steak, because Andy thought that might be a good question The Shark had never been asked before. Andy was right. Greg had never been asked that question before. He gave me a quizzical look that was probably reserved for morons.

'I don't think so, buddy.' As luck would have it, after the birth of Fergus, I ran into another Greg Norman. This time in the suburb of Jindalee, off the Centenary Highway that leads back into the city. Greg Norman paused as he introduced himself at the entrance to the surgery, almost as though he was waiting for one of us to say something derogatory or amusing.

'Hi, Greg Norman . . . how can I help you today?' Darlene was not at all interested in sports and the unusual name . . . Dr Greg Norman. It didn't even register, but this was a woman who failed to notice that she was standing next to Darren Lockyer, the captain of the Brisbane Broncos, at the dry-cleaners. Fergus had a nasty eye infection, full of gunk and pus, although Greg Norman, the doctor, seemed unimpressed. He told us that all Darlene had to do was squeeze some breast-milk in Fergus's eyes to make them better, although he gave us a prescription for some eye drops just to be sure. We never used the prescription. A couple of squirts of breastmilk and it cleared up like magic.

I thought about that amazing day, standing there with Greg Norman – the golfer, not the doctor – every time I drove my car along the main road past the course to our rented house, which had a media room, four bedrooms, and two huge bathrooms. It was way too big for the two of us, although with Fergus on the way we would soon be glad of that extra room. I watched with fascination in the weeks leading up to the birth as Darlene performed the nesting ritual, decorating the nursery with a large white cot and a change table borrowed from my sister. She sanded it back with a Black & Decker and repainted, wiping the sweat off her brow every time her huge extended tummy got in the way. Whenever I looked at her tummy I felt either vaguely guilty . . . *You did that to her, you bastard* . . . or vaguely proud . . . *you did that to her, you bastard.* I kept telling her to take it easy but she loved restoring furniture and was particularly enamoured with the importance of this task. There were star-shaped knobs for the draws and Fergus's name in blue and green emblazoned on pillows. The wardrobes were stacked with toys, baby jumpsuits, towels of every shape and size, and soft muslin cloths to use as covers when breastfeeding. Every night before she fell asleep she would be immersed in books with names like *Kidwrangling* or *What to Expect When You're Expecting.* Considering what I was in for I should have been reading them too.

Darlene has composed herself, fixed up her panda eyes in the rear-view mirror, and there is one last wave as she swings the car forwards onto the street and heads to work on that first day. A heavy winter fog is lifting across the valley below us and the air smells damp and sweet. Wattles with golden blossoms flower in the park nearby. There is no doubting her bravery or the sacrifices she is making for her family but it wouldn't be more than a few months later that the differences between men and women in this regard became glaringly obvious. We are out with friends when the conversation turns to work.

'Darlene works such long hours, sometimes twelve- or thirteen-hour days,' I said. 'It's incredible.' Darlene's mood towards me disintegrated over the course of the afternoon, and on the way home in the car she exploded with anger.

'All those women there, they thought I was a bad mother,' she said.

'Why would they think that?' I asked. 'I wanted them to know the sacrifices you are making. That I'm proud of you.'

'Well, if you're so proud of me, don't ever say that again.'

As the car engine fades into the distance and the garage door bangs shut I realise quite dramatically that my life will never be the same again. I am home alone at Ipswich with a six-month-old baby. My wife's tears have unnerved me for I am suddenly consumed by a crippling self-doubt. I'm reminded of a scene from *Seinfeld* where Kramer tells George that he has 'to listen to the little man' because the little man 'always knows'. George replies that the advice is lost on him because his little man 'was an idiot'. My little man, the voice in my head, is telling me that it's my fault that my wife is so upset. *If only you earned more money! What sort of a man are you, standing here holding a baby while your wife goes off to work? You need to put an end to this nonsense. It's time to man-up.*

As I was to discover, this feeling never really went away. Years later when my confidence was at an all time low I Googled 'stay-at-home dad'. I was looking for some advice from other men in my situation. Pretty soon I stumbled across a YouTube clip posted by an evangelical church in America. The preacher is sitting with his wife in front of a large audience and he's not like other preachers because he's young and hip with a cool haircut and denim-washed jeans, cracking jokes. His blonde-haired wife turns deadly serious and says stay-at-home dads can't provide for the needs of a child like a woman can, because it's not hard-wired in their brains.

'They think they are helping their kids out but they're not. How can they be when a woman can do the job so much better?' The crowd applauds. Some laughter. 'It's hard to respect a man who doesn't provide for his family.'

Her husband, the preacher, says, 'These guys would be well advised to stop playing at being Peter Pan. A stay-at-home dad is not a man.' The crowd cheers.

A shiver went up my spine.

5

DON'TS FOR WIVES

I must not become housebound. I must conquer my fear of heading out to do the grocery shopping with Fergus . . . alone.

There is much to fear. Andy had a horror story from the parents' room at Beaudesert Hospital, when his daughter's bottom had turned into something resembling a fire extinguisher, spraying an entire wall in a thin film of shit. He started dabbing at it with some baby wipes before packing up and fleeing the crime scene, still wracked by guilt for what the next parent would encounter when they ventured inside, not to mention the poor contract cleaners. Exploding nappies are one thing but I'm more concerned about regurgitation, which, based on percentages, is far more likely.

Everywhere we go with Fergus a spew cloth must be taken, draped over the shoulder in preparation for the inevitable spill. Liquid seems to pour out of him throughout the day. I was thinking about getting a lovely photo of Darlene and Fergus framed until I realised there was a long thin stream of white goo that had just come out of his mouth running down her blouse. She was so happy and oblivious to the mess.

And then there is the screaming. At home I've seen my happy contented baby turn in seconds from a perfect angel into a snarling pit bull. The culprit could be anything: reflux, sore gums, wind, or just plain tiredness. Over time I would become adept at spotting the symptoms for these ailments, although for the moment, like Mr Magoo bumbling around with a nappy bag on his shoulder, I'm clueless. The thought of embarrassing myself at the shops, of drawing attention to myself with a screaming baby at the checkout, of being one of those parents who can't control their child, fills me with dread, makes me sweat.

But before I can take on the grocery shopping I must at least make myself presentable to the good people of suburban Redbank Plains, where the Woolworths I plan on visiting is located. This means getting out of my pyjamas, having a shower and changing into some proper clothes. A simple enough task you might think but not, as I discover, when you're home alone with a six-month-old. I consider leaving Fergus in his bouncinette in front of the television, where he is happily watching a Baby Mozart DVD bought for him by his aunty. Colourful twirling shapes dance before his eyes accompanied by the maestro's classical tunes. But images of him choking to death when I return flood my mind and I think better of it. The comedian Roseanne Barr once said that she measured her success as a mum by whether her children were alive at the end of the day. It is wise advice.

I find I'm faced with these choices all the time, constantly weighing up levels of risk, of sprinting around corners and back again, of being terrified of leaving him alone. Instead I lug his bouncinette into the bathroom, making sure I can see him at all times except when the shampoo gets into my eyes. Already, I have seen him get into trouble so quickly – put a dead fly into his mouth, knock over a glass that he couldn't possibly reach that then smashes on the tiles, almost hang himself from a cord on the venetian blinds – with such breathtaking quickness that I'm half expecting him to have disappeared when I finally see again through the shampoo suds. In the days and months that follow, as Fergus learns how to crawl, then cruise, then walk, I struggle to even have a shower or get out of my pyjamas before Darlene gets home, yet at the end of the day I wonder how this is possible when there are just the two of us at home. The days seem painfully slow yet filled with the force of a mini hurricane.

As a joke Darlene buys me a present from Mary Ryan's Books at Milton called *Don'ts for Wives*. Subtle societal changes over the past one hundred years had turned a serious book published in 1913 into an object of amusement. Inside she highlighted a section of text where it was suggested by the author, whose first name is Blanche, that the woman of the house should always spend an hour freshening up her attire so as to put the husband in a better mood when he got home from work: 'Don't allow yourself to get into the habit of dressing carelessly when there is "only" your husband to see you. Depend upon it he has no use for faded tea-gowns and badly dressed hair, and he abhors the sight of curling pins as much as other men do. He is a man after all and if his wife does not take the trouble to charm him, there are plenty of other women who will.'

Call it a crisis of confidence, but, seeing the tables were turned and I was, metaphorically speaking, the good woman at home with the curling pins in my hair, it got me wondering about all the powerful, successful men with bulging pay packets that Darlene was mixing with during the day before coming home to a husband still dressed in his pyjamas. Perhaps they'd heard that her husband was a stay-at-home dad. After all, I am a man and I know how men think, mainly about sex every fifty-two seconds. In the eyes of some would-be predators an attractive woman with a husband who stays at home with the kids would be like a red rag to a bull. *A wimp at home*, I could hear them thinking, *maybe she's after a real man*.

One night she tells me about a businessman who's invited her to lunch at a fancy restaurant in the city under the pretence of discussing work. There is a condition on the offer: that it's just the two of them and she must make the booking.

Darlene wasn't sure what to do. Her little woman, the voice in her head, was telling her that maybe the businessman was making a subtle pass at her.

'A subtle pass!' I shouted in frustration as I took the curling pins out of my hair. 'Why didn't he just drop his pants?'

Darlene remained calm and pointed out to me that if she snubbed the businessman then the consequences for her work could be far reaching.

'This is a delicate matter. Perhaps he just wants to have lunch? Shouldn't I give him the benefit of the doubt? Why does this have to be so difficult?'

'The booking is the real key here,' I said as I moisturised my face and hands and tried to make myself more presentable. 'That's what's making you uneasy. It's what's making me uneasy. In fact, it makes me want to go around to his office and punch him in the nose. If you make the booking then he thinks you're sending him a signal. Game on for sleazebags! Worst-case scenario: he'll have too many red wines, put the moves on, and maybe even pour his heart out about how much he loves you. Then when you reject him he'll be bitter and twisted and won't give you the help you need anyway. If you complain about harassment he'll lie and tell everyone that you're the one who invited him to lunch. You made the first move. All because *you* made the booking.'

Darlene thought about it for a while as she sipped on some wine and heated the chicken stir-fry in the microwave. (These were the early days when I was determined to have dinner on the table when she came home from work. Now that we have two children my culinary delights stretch into the realms of baked beans on toast.

'Right. I think I understand,' she said about the business-man. 'So I'll get *him* to make the booking.'

On the weekend I drove to Mary Ryan's to purchase Blanche's twin edition: *Don'ts for Husbands*. I will have my revenge. It has a light blue cover, as opposed to the red one Darlene had given me. Seems the men in early 1900s Great Britain led a pretty cruisey life, smoking lots of cigarettes which they sometimes ashed on the carpet, going to men's clubs quite regularly to play cards and having a fondness for cheese: 'Don't insist on having gorgonzola or other strong smelling cheese on the table twice a day when you know the odour makes your wife feel ill, after all, it is a small thing to forgo in comparison with your wife's comfort.'

A few days later, on a Friday night, Darlene came home late after a work function. Work drinks and dinner had been arranged at the pub for a colleague leaving the office for an overseas posting. I heard the taxi pull up and the sound of her fumbling with the keys in the front door as she stumbled inside. When she climbed into bed beside me I could smell the alcohol from the vodka, lime and sodas she liked to drink. Then surprise, surprise, she started running her fingers through my hair and whispering sweet nothings in my ear.

'I really appreciate what you're doing with Fergus,' she slurred. 'You're a wonderful, sexy stay-at-home daddy-man.' Angry thoughts at being woken up at such a late hour quickly dissipated, replaced by primeval logic common to all married men when presented with sexual opportunity by their wife, especially not long after the birth of your first child, mainly: under no condition are you to waste it! Weeks, if not months, might pass before your wife would be consumed by such madness again. As I turned to reciprocate Darlene's advances I was met with a blast of garlic-laden breath from the mushroom risotto she had eaten, which, when combined with the alcohol, made my eyes water. It was all I could do not to grab my nostrils or demand that she go fetch me a gasmask. It probably wasn't as bad as gorgonzola but suddenly I understood the subtle message Blanche was trying to convey.

After my world-record-breaking short shower I dress in cargo pants and a polo shirt and give Fergus his bottle so he is nice and relaxed. I'm already quite adept at holding it at the right angle to stop bubbles forming and so prevent wind. After his bottle, just to be sure, I jiggle him on my knee and lean him forward, patting his back, and I can feel the burp coming out of him. Of this skill I am also becoming quite proud, calling myself the burp master and imagining myself winning the gold medal for this particular task over more fancied female rivals at the baby Olympics. I am determined my first mission to the shops alone will be a successful one, so I put a lot of thought into the ammunition I'll be using in my black Bjorn Again nappy bag, bought for me by my sister for Christmas. There's formula, a spare bottle, nappies, Bonjela ointment for his gums, baby wipes, zinc-based rash cream, a spare change of clothes. Fergus is also addicted to his dummy and I have a few replacements just in case he drops one. My mother was horrified when she saw Fergus sucking on a dummy for the first time.

'You may as well give him some chewing gum,' she said. 'It looks disgusting.' It started not long after he was born. The only way we could get him to stop crying was to put one in his mouth. I can't even remember who was the first of us to try it, but it worked. After a few weeks we succumbed to peer pressure and got rid of the dummy, tried to wean him off it, until the paediatrician told us that we'd be crazy not to keep using something that worked.

'Every baby is different,' he said when I told him about the criticism. I put the spare dummies in my nappy bag and squeeze it shut using two hands before I sling it over my shoulder. In time I learn to love my nappy bag, the contents of which change as Fergus grows and develops. Darlene even discovers a company in America called Diaper Dude, which makes stylish nappy bags for men. You can carry your laptop and your baby's bottles. So I'm not alone. Out there in the world there must be thousands of men like me. Even Brad Pitt has one. After a few months sippy cups filled with real milk or tap water will replace the formula powder. There'll be nutritious snacks: yoghurts, sandwiches cut into tiny quarters, sultanas, Cruskits. In another section will be Hot Wheels cars and small wind-up toys to distract him if I'm forced to wait anywhere for a length of time. I learn to be prepared.

At this hour of the day, mid-morning, there is a window of opportunity between sleeps. I figure a baby with a full tummy will be more contented than one without. I pack Fergus into my Ford Laser, start up the car and head for the shops. I realise with joy when I swing into the car park that I can now slip into the 'parents with prams' spot without fear of reprisal. At this particular shopping centre there are two such spots and one of them is free. In keeping with these politically correct times the prominent red effigy of the pram spray-painted on the bitumen is being pushed by an androgynous figure that could be either a man or a woman. Before children I hated the parents with prams spots, especially at Christmas when parks were at a premium.

'Who do you people with children think you are?' I said to Andy once, making sure Sally was nowhere within earshot. 'Do you think you're better than everyone else, that you deserve special treatment just because you have children? Next we'll be giving you special stickers to put on your windscreen.'

'It's not that we're more deserving,' replied Andy. 'It's just so much easier and safer to get in and out of the car when it's nearer to the door, to stop the kids running around all over the place. One day you'll understand and be grateful for them, just like I am. If you can get one, that is.'

Andy was right. People who don't have prams or even small children like to steal these spots and securing one is always much harder than finding a normal park. Parking in a parents with pram spot when you don't have babies or toddlers is the perfect untraceable crime. At best it's morally wrong, but certainly not against the law, at least not yet. You could get fined for parking in a disabled spot without a permit. But you couldn't for parking in parents with prams spot. Soon I was demanding the death penalty for those who encroach upon this sacred ground, usually, as I would discover over the next few years, university students in Hyundais, tradesmen in utes, people with interstate numberplates in campervans, and elderly people who like the proximity to the shop's front doors but are not so far gone physically that they can qualify for a disabled parking sticker. I can see why they do it, because I know why I did it.

Just like the disabled park, they appear before you much like an apparition and it's all you can do to resist their siren-like call, especially when they are located so close to all the action. *I'll only be a few minutes. No one will notice.* But people do notice. People with kids notice. I notice. Many months later I felt so strongly on the subject I ask a young tradie getting out of his ute where his kids are. One arm is covered in tattoos. He is sipping on an iced coffee. He takes one look at me with my nappy bag and folding Prego pram.

'Get a life, fuckhead,' he says before wandering off.

I walk slowly to the side of the car and extract Fergus from his baby capsule, wrapping him in a light swaddling before heading through the automatic doors of Woolworths. I start looking for one of those trolleys Darlene has told me about with a built-in baby capsule and holding straps so I can lay him down facing me. There are a few available and they all look reasonably clean. I am not worried about him picking up germs.

Author Dr Karl Kruszelnicki recommends that visitors to hospital put a pinkie into the mouths of newborns to stimulate the immune system. Even though he has a fondness of Hawaiian shirts, which always makes me suspicious of anyone, it sounds like good logical advice, and I'm determined to be logical in my parenting instead of hysterical. Plus, I've read *Buddhism for Mothers* and am trying to put into practice the meditation techniques to stop the worrying. For the moment, in my mind at least, germs are good things to be sought out and embraced, not controlled or destroyed. I figure a shopping-centre trolley should be jam-packed with the kind I'm after. I'm also determined not to become one of those parents who lather their kids and their hands in alcohol-based Dettol gels that are becoming so popular. I'm going to let Fergus play in the mud, roll in the dirt, get as filthy as he pleases. Of course, I hadn't yet experienced the horrors of hand, foot and mouth disease, and conjunctivitis and other horrible bugs and viruses with names like Slap Face because it made his cheeks go all red. And when he did start playing in the dirt under the house I noticed that there was a cat poo there and worried that he would get toxoplasmosis like that Scottish bloke in *Trainspotting* gets from a kitten and his head swells up like a balloon and his brain explodes.

Fergus seems happy enough as I begin trolling the aisles, starting as I always do with fruit and vegetables and making my way through the rest of the store. I see another man who has a baby in his trolley and a toddler running about wildly through the aisles. He flags me as a brother in arms and we nod at each other in silent recognition. This happens from time to time, as fellow stay-at-home dads or other men pushing prams pass me on the street or at the shops. Nick says that if I went shopping at New Farm then it might mean something completely different, especially if I had bananas in my trolley. About a year later I see a man struggling with his children near a Thomas the Tank Engine coin-operated ride at Indooroopilly Shopping Centre. He has a baby in his pram and twin daughters aged about three. As I pass with Fergus in my pram he says to them, 'Oh, we can't play with Thomas the Tank Engine . . . we can't use it because this man here wants to use it for his little boy.'

'Oh, no, I'm not going to use it,' I say, trying not to sound condescending. I think that parents who let their kids loose on such rides at shopping centres are suckers, asking for trouble as it opens up a whole new front on the battleground. There are already enough distractions at the shops. I know that once Fergus experiences the two-dollar delights of the gentle rolling action and flashing lights he would want it every time, over and over. It isn't going to happen. I will never let my guard down. Never.

'We're just on our way to the elevator.'

'Yes . . . this . . . man . . . wants . . . to . . . use . . . it,' he says again, slowly, with pitiful, pleading eyes. His daughters look at me to see how I'll react. They look at me then they look back at their father.

'Ah, yes. That's right,' I say.

His children accept his explanation and the man scurries them away, whispering, 'Thanks, champ. You're a lifesaver.'

Of course, Fergus has heard the whole thing too and suddenly I am the one with the problem. I can't explain to Fergus the concept of the white lie, he hasn't even learnt to lie properly himself yet, and so soon he is yelping with delight as the Thomas the Tank Engine whirrs up and down . . . toot, toot. As I stand there I feel very much like the village idiot, hoping nobody will see me, my head held down in shame.

At Woolworths I hear the stay-at-home dad yell at his son, 'Hands off the bloody pasta, Jadyn.' It's like I'm looking into my future, for Darlene and I are already discussing possible plans for a sibling for Fergus. In fact, as soon as you pump out your first child the questioning starts: 'Are you going to have another?' Peter Costello, the Treasurer, is on the television saying that parents should have one for the father, one for the mother and one for the country. The implication seems to be that it is selfish to have just one, which I think is rather awful for those parents who, for whatever reason, could only have one. And what about those parents who have to adopt? It must really make them mad. And what if we couldn't have another? The first time round had been so difficult. Shopping with one baby was scary enough. Would I be able to handle two, especially when one is no longer constrained inside the pram?

Young Jadyn is gradually tearing Woolworths to pieces, his shrieks of excitement growing louder and louder. The slap,

slap, slap of his bare feet echo around the store. Some of the older shoppers are casting furtive glances at each other, for which the meaning is obvious: *In my day, we would have given that kid a good smack on the bottom.* Would I end up with the same look on my face as this dad, whose creased expression conveyed a mixture of anger, worry and embarrassment, if we have another?

'Now come on, Jadyn. Come on, mate. Put the chocolates down. You just wait till we get home.'

My shopping trip, though, couldn't have gone better. As I go through the checkout armed with my green recycling bags and pay my bill I am overcome with a tremendous satisfaction that comes with a job well done. I have done a shop by myself with a six-month-old and have not made a fool of myself or managed to harm my son in any way. No one is casting aspersions in my direction. A grandmotherly type has already leaned over and started making cooing noises at him as she tickles him with a long bony finger.

'Adorable,' she says to me. Fergus is lying there in his capsule staring at me, smiling at the customers, smiling at the lady with the bony finger, blinking at the bright lights, taking it all in.

'This is my first shop,' I say to the gangly teenage girl at the checkout.

'What?'

'This is my first shop. With my baby.'

'Oh . . . yeah . . . great,' she says, rolling her eyes.

Over the coming years there will be numerous exchanges and incidents at checkout counters. Tantrums as the children don't get what they want. Years later I make the mistake of promising Fergus a WALL-E the robot figurine if he behaves himself but when he goes to pick one out he wants three instead of one. Then he throws a fit worthy of a world championship wrestler. As he gyrates on the floor my mind flips through the range of options open to me: One, I can give him the figurines. Two, I can run out of the shop with him under my arm. Three, I can give him nothing and proceed to the checkout.

It soon becomes obvious that the moment, which I have been avoiding up till now, has arrived. If I fail to check this bad behaviour at the start he will almost certainly end up being a mass murderer; one bad behaviour leading to another and another and finally jail and oblivion. So I stand in the line for the checkout looking above the heads of everyone in the shop, not making eye contact with anyone, while Fergus hurls abuse at me, squirming in my arms, slipping through them onto the ground.

'Leave me alone,' he screams. 'Don't touch me.' My heart starts to race and time seems to stand still as I imagine I'm somewhere else and that if I can just get through this nightmare and emerge the other side we'll be better people, both me and my son. An old lady rescues me. She offers me her place in the line.

'We've all been there,' she says. I love this old woman. I want to hug her and smother her face in kisses. Perhaps she helped me because she could see that I was trying, that I wasn't giving in to the bad behaviour.

There are other times when I am the super dad of the supermarket. An old man comes up to me and says, 'You're a great father. That child of yours is so beautifully behaved.' Or the time that Fergus says to everyone within earshot, 'I love you, Daddy.' I can feel the hearts of the mums about me melt. Luckily they weren't there when he told me in the car not ten minutes later that he hated me. I soon learn, though, that the level of difficulty increases when you can no longer keep them in the trolley. Once on the ground you need to keep them actively involved, getting them to help you with shopping lists, praising them for good behaviour. This is where, despite all your great parenting, at some point they will streak off down an aisle and you'll worry that you'll never see them again. And through it all you have to keep a sense of calmness about you, for if they sense that you are losing control, that you're about to lose it, that's when they will lose it too.

Outside in the car park I perform a delicate series of manoeuvres to get the milk and eggs and other groceries onto the back seat without the trolley, with Fergus still inside, either smashing into the bumper, scratching the doors or worse, rolling down the slight incline and out of my grasp. Next I take the trolley over to the docking station where all good citizens leave their trolleys because, even though Fergus is still a baby, I want him to learn that these types of unselfish behaviours are what separate the good citizens from the bad ones, the civilised creatures from the beasts. It's not good enough to rely on the staff to clean up after you, because Nick was a trolley horse when he was at uni, the first of many part-time jobs from which he was fired for laziness and dereliction of duty. He spent most of the time smoking near the back steps while chatting up the checkout chicks. If Nick was on duty then my trolley could sit there for hours and perhaps bump into a car, causing a nasty scratch.

Now that Fergus is out of the trolley, and before I put him in the car, I check that my car keys are in my pocket. On the evening news recently there was a story about a mother who'd left the keys in the ignition and locked her baby in her four-wheel drive. A baby can die within minutes in the sub-tropical South East Queensland heat and the mother, in a panic, had managed to attract the attention of a plumber – perhaps he'd parked in the parents with prams spot next to her. He attacked the windscreen with a sledgehammer. I don't know what they make windows out of these days but he couldn't break it. It just wouldn't shatter. Luckily the fire brigade arrived and saved the day, prising the doors open with the jaws-of-life. It is an example of the sort of things that can go wrong. All this worrying about car keys makes me lose focus on what I should be focusing on: getting my baby into his capsule without whacking his head into the side of the car. I hear the thud and he looks at me with pleading, searching eyes: *What did you do that for?* He starts to cry and I can see a small red indentation on his perfect head near his eye. Over and over again I say, 'I'm sorry, mate. I'm so sorry.' I keep touching the indentation hoping to rub it away, but already I can see that there will be a bruise. He stops crying after a minute or two and I'm wondering if I should take him to the doctor. *Don't be like those first-time parents who react to everything,* I tell myself. *It's a little whack in the face, an accident. These things happen. It's not like he'll have brain damage. Surely, he won't have brain damage.* Already I'm thinking about what Darlene will say tonight when she gets home.

The petrol gauge warning light turns orange and starts flashing. This is an unexpected hiccup in my plans but there is no need for me to panic as there is a petrol station off the main road. At the bowser I don't want all those fumes getting inside the car so I make sure the windows are done up nice and tight. I check my pocket again and make sure I have the car keys. *But what about the increase in temperature in a car that's been shut up?* We're in the shade under the roof of the service station. *Could it harm his little developing brain to be left inside for a few minutes?* And now I'm faced with another dilemma: *Should I leave Fergus in the car or take him with me when I go to pay the bill?*

The front counter behind the sliding doors is only ten metres away. There aren't many people in the queue. I could be in and out in a minute or two. My mind hums like a computer, assessing the various dangers that could lead to the harm of my child. Mum told me that she used to leave me on the back seat of the car in my bassinet while she did the shopping. She parked the car under a tree and left the window open. As long as she could see the car she wasn't overly concerned. There were no baby capsules in those days. The bassinet was strapped into the back with a seat belt.

'Didn't you have car thieves back then,' I said.

'I guess we never worried about stuff like that,' she said.

I imagine myself clinging to the bonnet of the Laser as a thief drives off with Fergus, because these days we are definitely worried about stuff like that. The thief is braking and I'm sliding off onto the concrete before he drives over my shattered body. Even though I recover from my life-threatening injuries and learn to talk again through a voice recorder, Darlene refuses to speak to me and Fergus lives the rest of his life with a car thief who raises him as one of his own. With a sigh of resignation I unclip the capsule and lean in to the car, which is low to the ground and so I have to be almost on my knees to get down and lift him out. This time it is me who whacks his head on the window frame as I reach in to grab him. Soon I will have a bruise on the back of my head just as bad as the one on the front of his.

I have watched enough episodes of *Supernanny* to know that I must maintain the routine if I am to survive. If I am in any doubt Darlene has written an elaborate one down for me from her favourite book, *Kidwrangling*, and stuck it on the fridge with a magnet. Looking at it makes me giddy. How on earth am I going to pull this off on my own?

Fergus wakes up.
Feed: breakfast (formula and maybe a taste of solids).
Play.
Possible sleep.
Feed: morning tea (formula and maybe a taste of solids).

Play.

Sleep.

Feed: lunch (formula and a taste of solids).

Play.

Sleep.

Feed: afternoon tea (formula and maybe a taste of solids).

Play.

Possible catnap if there are tired signs.

'Arsenic hour': a restful activity.

Feed: dinner (a taste of solids and a drink of water).

Play (may be longer than usual, but watch for tired signs).

Bath.

Drink: formula.

Night-time ritual.

Sleep: about 7pm.

Already I have deviated from the routine. And I've made a rookie error by letting Fergus fall asleep in the car on the way home and now he's grumpy and hungry and AWAKE. I am about to learn the hard way that letting your child fall asleep in the car for a few minutes on the way back from the shops is a parenting disaster of epic proportions – it is almost impossible to get them back to sleep again when you transfer them into their cot. You try, of course, but the trip from the car seat to the cot, with the unbuckling, the opening of the house doors with keys, the clomping of noisy shoes down the hallway, always wakes them up. Their eyes snap open and suddenly you're holding Chucky the doll in your arms. There is a price to pay for missing that hour-plus morning sleep. It throws the whole day out of whack and leads to tantrums that make Tasmanian devils look like good house pets.

To stop such things from happening I learn to open the car window so the wind in his face will keep him awake or reach around when I can, keeping my eyes on the road – parents make wonderful contortionists – and tickle his feet through the material of the baby jumpsuit. I'm a big fan of the baby jumpsuit. It makes me wonder why all of us, adults included don't get around in them. They make sense: easy to put on, easy to take off, easy to wash, no need for shoes. Jerry Seinfeld says it's why people from the future or aliens in movies always wear silver jumpsuits. Smart people from advanced civilisations or other planets have worked this out before us. On the weekends Darlene will struggle to dress Fergus in designer outfits from Oshkosh and Pumpkin Patch, especially if we're going to visit Andy and Sally.

'You're not putting him in the jumpsuit,' she'll shout if I'm given the task of dressing him. Around the home it's okay but not when we go out and other mothers will be judging the quality of the outfit. I couldn't care less about the looks of other mothers and the quality of the outfit. If it's practical and he's not going to freeze or boil to death, then it's for me.

Fergus is crying from tiredness but I'm still a novice and think maybe he's just hungry, so I place him in his high chair and give him, as per the routine on the fridge, a taste of solids: a type of rice pudding. I'm speeding up the routine; I've put my finger on the fast-forward button and skipped straight to lunch trying to erase about two hours from the day. It would have been better to drive around in the car for an hour or so until he had his rest. You can improvise with the routine but you can't cheat. He sits there screaming at me, his little skinny legs dangling from beneath the silver-coloured tray.

The high chair is an expensive Italian model with a black leather seat purchased by Nanna and Grampi as a present before Fergus's birth. It is Italian because Grampi is a car enthusiast who owns a silver Maserati with black seats and has purchased a red Alfa Romeo GT, both designed by a man called Giorgetto. They both agreed that if Italians can make cars of such beauty then they can also make great high chairs. I thought this made sense until it occurred to me that Grampi was also on a first-name basis with his mechanic. The high chair is indeed a thing of beauty but the leather turns out to be totally impractical as all the food that spills out Fergus's mouth gets caught in the crevices and starts to smell. It involves hours of careful cleaning to get rid of the collateral damage. Turns out the Italians make crappy high chairs but I persevere with it because it was expensive and Nanna and Grampi will be upset if I replace it with the minimalist design from IKEA that Sally has. Its smooth uncomplicated lines don't allow for any food to be caught and can be hosed off in the backyard in seconds for easy convenience.

I put around Fergus's neck a plastic bib with an inbuilt splash tray moulded at the bottom to catch any spillage. While impressive looking it also fails to catch any of the mountains of food that come spilling down his chin. Sometimes after he's finished eating I feel that I may as well have poured the contents on his head, as I've gotten very little into his mouth and the results look pretty much like that's what I did anyway. After several false starts, where I'm parrying with the spoon like one of the three musketeers, I manage to score a bullseye and get the rice pudding in his mouth. His eyes spin back in his head like the symbols on a poker machine and the pudding dribbles down his chin. He screams even louder. I can't really blame him. I've tasted it and it is bland and disgusting. That night I tell Darlene about my trouble with getting Fergus to eat the bland tasteless solids she has provided me with and she tosses me a baby cookbook. She isn't impressed with the critical tone to my voice.

'Well if you're so bloody concerned, why don't you make your own?'

'You know what, I think I will,' I say confidently, determined to be a stay-at-home dad who can match it with the Donna Hays of this world. Soon I'm stewing apples and carrots and zucchini that I have chopped up in the blender and reduced to a sloppy mess in the saucepan, freezing the leftovers for use during the week.

'I'll show her,' I say over and over again to myself for inspiration. Of course, I get sick of this after a few days as it seems totally unrealistic and way too much work. After all, I'm a practical person who loves Bonds jumpsuits. Even those late-night ads of people having so much fun in their blanket

Snuggies are starting to appeal to me. I've seen a lady at the shops wearing one held together with a belt and I wanted to congratulate her on her brave purchase. So there must be a way to streamline the fresh-food process, which in the world of men usually means get someone else to do it.

I discover on the internet a company called Little Tummy Tucker, which makes nutritious fresh meals from a commercial kitchen in New Farm. I order them online and a courier van delivers them to my door, two weeks' worth of tasty meals that would have taken me hours to make, and all packaged neatly in a styrofoam box covered in ice packs. I get a discount if I return the box, which gives me a good excuse to take Fergus for a stroll around New Farm Park where there is a lovely walking track near the river. Afterwards, I spread out a picnic blanket and enjoy the company of my baby, resisting the urge to lather him in sunscreen the moment a speckle of sunlight lands on his pristine white skin. The mothers around me are all doing this, plastering little faces and arms with 30 plus as their babies wriggle about in their arms. Why does it annoy me that they are being so fastidious? I feel like standing up and shouting: 'For Christ's sake, what are you so concerned about? A little bit of sun is not going to hurt them. We're in the bloody shade!'

I find that having excuses to go out is an important part of being a stay-at-home dad. There is a desire to grin and bear it as the monotonous routine of looking after children plays out day after day. It takes a lot of energy to pack up the pram and the nappy bag and drive to a park and there are all sorts of things that can wrong when you are away from the safety of the mothership, but once you're out in the fresh open air with your baby it's amazing how it revitalises your spirits. I think this is why mothers have mothers' groups. As I have no invitations to any mothers' group and no other men to hang out with it puts me at a distinct disadvantage.

I didn't know it then, but already the isolation was starting to grind me down.

6

MOMENTS TO CELEBRATE

I learn that being a good stay-at-home dad means learning to be proactive, to act quickly to the signs or even before there are signs, checking his nappy, making sure he isn't hungry or tired. When I see him rubbing his eyes I start the sleep routine we have established together: putting him in his tiny sleeping bag, drawing the blinds, holding him in the cradle position and walking about the house singing Powderfinger songs until Fergus's eyes start to droop. *Don't be too quick to get him into the cot*, my little man, the voice in my head, warns me. It's all about patience, not being in a rush to get him down. Round and round the inside of the house I go; if the floor wasn't so hard there would be a well-worn trail resembling the one elephants use when moving through the jungle. Once his eyes are closed and his breathing deepens I still count to one hundred just to be sure, and even then my anticipation rises that he might wake up and we'll have to start all over again. I lay him on his back and hope that those eyes don't crack open because there will be some heavy-duty screaming if they do.

Soon I can tell the difference between a tired cry and a hungry cry and a cry of pain, and the amazing thing is that his are different to those of other children. My nostrils can make out the slightest waft of a poo in his nappy, which is also different to other people's children. I'm like one of those penguins that can find their chicks among thousands of others. I am also the rash master. As soon as anything resembling a reddish blotch appears on his bottom or crease on his skin I attack it with zinc cream and powder. I seem to have a relentless zeal when it comes to such things. It occurs to me that maybe men are better than females when it comes to dealing with rashes – after all, we play football in the mud and rain and take to wearing wet board shorts in the summer at the beach. As a consequence we know how important it is to keep on top of such things. A fungal infection between the legs can quickly turn very nasty indeed. Men know how painful it can be and how to treat it. I can't remember hearing about a girl getting jock rot. I'm quite proud of this theory until Andy points out to me that women get thrush, especially pregnant women.

'Oh,' I say.

My rash-master theory might have been blown out of the water but there is no doubting my new-found confidence in my abilities as the nurturer. What does that preacher's wife on YouTube know anyway? My competitive juices flow on perfecting difficult tasks. I am now an expert at dismantling and installing a car seat in any vehicle you care to point me in the direction of, including a taxi. I can change a nappy with breathtaking speed, sometimes using only one hand. Let's see that preacher's wife take me on at that. I have developed a theory on looking after Fergus that is helping me cope: I will not ever try to do anything that might distract from the needs of my baby; I will not try to read the paper; I will not try to watch television; I will resist the urge of the Foxtel ads and not get it installed even if it is half price. I discover that if I push aside any selfish thoughts about what I want to do during the day and focus entirely on him then my job is so much simpler and easier. It helps with the anger and the resentment that simmer beneath the surface on the bad days when everything seems to go wrong. Sally tells me that what I'm suffering from here is called 'burnt chop syndrome', where a mother puts her needs second to the needs of her family. The children and the husband get the best chops. The mother accepts the burnt one. Lucky for me then that Darlene is a vegetarian. I also reduce my day to achieving one attainable goal. It might be a phone call to the ISP to fix the broadband. It might be to do a load of washing, to vacuum the floor, to go to the shops and do the grocery shopping. At the very best I might assign myself two jobs to complete during the day. I see women battling under the strain of doing several tasks, knowing that they are setting themselves up for failure. I don't need failure; I need victories and small ones will do just fine.

Six months ago I had trouble remembering to get the car serviced. Now there are endless meals to prepare, bottles to make involving formula measurements and microwaves and sterilisation, immunisations to remember every few months, doctors to see when he breaks out in a series of nasty-looking spots or his temperature soars, schools to book him into because everyone is telling me that the best schools have waiting lists and you won't get in unless you registered early. He was not even a week old when I put him on the waiting list for the school I attended in the city. There were hundreds on it already. And don't forget childcare, they warn. Even if you are not planning on childcare for a while, it's difficult to secure good spots.

I put Fergus's name on several waiting lists at childcare centres. Someone is making money out of all this because hundreds of dollars fly out of my wallet – later only one of the several centres where I put his name down will offer us a place. I don't need childcare just yet anyway. I'm proud of the fact that my motherly instincts have become honed over months of constant practice, of sticking to a routine, of having no one else to rely on during the day but me – even though, as a man, my instinct when Fergus falls over is to dust him off and tell him to get on with it. Instead, I am conscious of the need to be nurturing, to make the appropriate coos and give him lots of cuddles. I've read that kids learn empathy from copying their mothers. I'm a poor substitute for Darlene when she's at work but it doesn't mean I'm not going to try. My child is going to be dripping with empathy.

Every time Fergus goes to sleep it is a moment to celebrate. Then I wonder about all the washing and cleaning that needs to be done and all the bills that have to be paid. Just because I'm at home it doesn't mean I can now sit on the couch and watch DVDs of famous Wallaby victories over the All Blacks. I have to clean the house to Darlene's exacting standards, which are much higher than my exacting standards. When I first moved out of home, my new roommate, who was a lot older than me and an experienced renter, took me into the bathroom and told me quite bluntly that I wasn't pulling my weight in the house when it came to cleaning. He wasn't going to stand for it anymore.

'Can you see what's wrong with the bathroom?' I thought the bathroom looked fine. 'All this fucking mould,' he said, pointing to the tiles. 'I'm sick of being the one to clean it up.' I'd never noticed it before; in fact, I thought the moss and algae gave the bathroom a kind of rainforest feel but I didn't tell him that. I apologised and told him I'd get right onto it. The next minute I was using good old elbow grease with a scrubbing brush and bleach.

'And when you've done that, we'll have a chat about the dunny,' he said.

My first attempts at cleaning the house after Darlene had gone to work were so time consuming and clumsy that I knew I'd have to come up with an alternative before the hard work killed me; meaning I had to get someone else to do it. The hiring of Lynda the cleaning lady solved this problem for a while until her husband got a job in Rockhampton and I was back in the shit again, literally. She was followed by two girls who turned up in short pants and tight singlets sent around by an agency I found in the Yellow Pages. It was one of those agencies that say the people in their employ love doing housework. The sight of two scantily clad females running around cleaning my house made me uneasy. I think I made them uneasy as well, standing there watching them with a baby on my hip. Luckily the two girls discovered they didn't actually like doing housework and disappeared, much to the annoyance of the business owner who had sent them.

Thinking I could save money by paying someone by the hour I replaced them with a much older Italian woman who didn't make me feel uneasy; in fact, she didn't make me feel anything, except angry. She hardly did any cleaning at all. She'd take out a thermos of coffee and sandwiches and start having little picnics while I fumed about the extra money she was costing me. I was trying to work out how to fire her when Lynda decided to return to Brisbane and my cleaning problems were solved again.

Lynda was a wonder-woman who would climb up and clean the dust off ceiling fans, finding dirt in places where other cleaning women feared to tread. Her son had played with the Brisbane Broncos and we could discuss the finer points of Rugby League and Wayne Bennett's coaching while she vacuumed and scrubbed. Evidence of her toughness was the fact she turned up for work with a fractured wrist. Lynda made me look good because she kept the house clean and that meant Darlene was happy. And Fergus loved her. She had an amazing ability to be able to clean while entertaining Fergus at the same time, giving him little jobs to do without breaking her stride. He would hold a little cleaning rag and trot around after her. He loved her so much that I invited her to babysit him on the weekend so Darlene and I could go to the movies. She burst into tears.

'You really trust me that much?' she asked. Suddenly I had a great cleaner and a great babysitter who knew Fergus's routine and adored spending time with him. Ask any mother, these people are almost impossible to find. They can't be found in the Yellow Pages, or in 'hired help' ads. One day, if you're lucky, they walk into your life. And if they do make sure you never tell anyone about them because a precious commodity like this must be kept a secret. That is why they are so hard to find because mothers never tell anyone about them. If they do let slip, there is an unwritten code that forbids you from ever asking for their number. And, of course, one day they can walk back out of your life again. Lynda's husband got another job, this time in Townsville, and she was gone again. I was this close to falling on my knees and sobbing, 'Please, Lynda, please don't go.' By that time, though, all money in the budget for such precious help was gone. She would not, and could not, be replaced. I would have to cope on my own.

Cleaning and babysitting is one thing but the laundry is mine alone. Strangely enough, washing is something I find quite relaxing. I enjoy hanging out the whites and the colours on a warm sunny day. I find the whole process quite soothing. I would put Fergus in his bouncinette and sing songs to him and talk while I'm pegging up the clothes. The trouble begins when he learns to crawl and doesn't want to be in the bouncinette. He wants to scoot along the concrete, taking the skin off his knees. He crawls with remarkable speed, and always towards the garden shed in the back corner where I've seen a king brown snake and a red-back spider. As he crawls he'll stop and put all kinds of things in his mouth too. I caught him seconds away from making a meal of a snail and the droppings of a possum. It reminded me of looking after a puppy, such was his determination to chew on everything that came into his field of vision.

While I like hanging out the washing I'm not very good at folding it up or ironing it. I simply stuff the clean sheets and towels into cupboards until the doors start to bulge. Darlene discovers them and shouts, 'I can't believe it!' Nothing can help me here unless I bring in someone to fold and iron, and there isn't nearly enough money for that on a regular basis. Soon Darlene underlines another passage in *Don'ts for Wives* and leaves it on my pillow: 'Don't permit yourself to forget for a single instant that nothing is more annoying to a tired man than the sight of unfinished laundry work.'

I'm putting Fergus's plastic plate and bowl in the sink when I hear a sickening thud. In a Houdini-esque act he has unclipped the straps crisscrossing his chest and fallen out of the Italian-designed high chair. I spin around and expect to see his brains

spilling out over the hard tiles. I pick him up and he is screaming with fright, going red in the face. I rock and cradle him
and pray to God that he'll be okay as a huge lump comes
up on his forehead and starts to turn a deep shade of purple. It's very hard to describe the feeling when you have hurt
your child, especially when it's the second time you've done
it within the space of a few weeks. Even though the bang on
the head during that first trip to the shops healed remarkably
quickly, suffice to say I wanted to turn into Superman and
spin the earth backwards to make everything all right again.
If I could have turned back time then I would have put myself
in harm's way, taken the blow, taken a thousand blows.

The doctor at the surgery where I rushed him seemed
unimpressed with this injury. He nodded his head slowly
when I told him that Fergus was our first child.

'He'll have a nasty bump on his head, but he's fine. Kids are
pretty tough you know. We handle them gently but they're built
like Mack Trucks.' My mum, when I told her, said accidents
like that came with the territory. She said my older brother
Colin had fallen on his head several times when he was a baby.

'Your brother was always getting up on the kitchen bench
and trying to get out windows. He turned out fine, didn't he?'
I thought that was debatable. Living with my older brother
was like living with a stuntman. He was forever building
ramps and riding skateboards and bicycles over them, swing-
ing and falling out of trees, landing on his head, knocking
himself out. I remember finding him under the house one day
smashing all the spare tiles for the roof of the house.

'Why are you doing this?' I asked him. 'Dad's going to kill you.'

'I don't know,' he replied.

'What about me, was I climber?' I asked Mum. 'Did I fall on my head a lot?'

'No, but you did walk under the fence at the elephant enclosure at Bullen's African Lion Safari Park when you were a toddler.'

'How come you've never told me that before? What the hell happened?'

'Well, no one noticed you were missing at first. You were just sitting there on the ground, playing quietly.'

'But what about the elephants, what if one of them had sat on me?'

'They didn't seem to notice you either.' It occurred to me that parenting in the seventies must have been a breeze. You shopped while you left the baby in the car and didn't stress when your child walked under the fence into an elephant enclosure.

A curious habit emerges on a Friday night after Fergus is asleep. As soon as Darlene walks in the door from work, I immediately start talking. Yap, yap, yap. I also have a beer in my hand. It's Friday night and she's home for the weekend so in my mind it's time for a little celebration: Crack open the champagne. It's party time! Darlene seems quite taken aback by my sudden willingness to talk when every other day of the week she either finds me already asleep on the couch, still in my pyjamas, sometimes on my back snoring in Fergus's nursery, still in my pyjamas, or staring like a zombie at *CSI Miami* on television, unable to communicate, still in my pyjamas. She usually wakes me up and squeezes the information out of me about the activities of the day.

'Did Fergus have his sleeps today?' 'What did he have to eat?' 'How many poos did he do?' 'What is that large lump on the front of his head?' A mumbled, 'Yeah, it was fine,' just doesn't cut it. She'll poke and prod me and sometimes it leads to arguments because I'm tired and just want to be left alone. Fergus has sucked the patience and understanding out of me much like he sucks milk from his bottle. I don't have any time for her. This happens on Monday, Tuesday, Wednesday and Thursday. But here is the strange flipside. Even though I'm up for a chat on Friday she does not want to talk to me. She's had a hard week at work. She wants to put her feet up on the couch, take in *Better Homes and Gardens* and forget about her troubles.

'We can talk about Fergus on the weekend,' she says. I start getting upset that she's not listening to me and she responds by saying, 'Now you know how I feel.'

I talk to Nick about this and he comes up with a theory as he loves coming up with theories. Nick says, according to his research, a woman needs to speak twenty thousand words a day and a man about half that number. He deduces that because I haven't spoken much to Darlene during the week, or actually anyone for that matter except a toddler, by the time

Friday rolls around I'm like a dam about to burst, and it all comes gushing out. Darlene, on the other hand, is tired from a busy week. She's used up all her words at work; she's way over her quota after all the meetings and crisis management dealings with staff and just wants to zone out.

'There's your problem right there, mate,' he announces, sounding quite pleased with himself. 'She becomes just like a man, just like you!' I look for signs of weakness in his argument but I have to admit it makes pretty good sense.

'Okay, it's a good theory, but what's the solution?'

'I've got three words for you, my friend, three words that will go part of the way to solving your little problem. Soon you won't care about talking to Darlene at the end of the working week.'

'Well, what are they? What are your three words?'

'Friday night football.'

It is when we go to the car dealer that I realise I have a real problem telling other men I am a stay-at-home dad. After a nasty scare on the highway when my brakes locked and I nearly crashed into the car in front of me, I have decided the Ford Laser is not safe enough transport for our baby. My transformation into a western suburbs' housewife will be complete with the purchase of a four-wheel-drive Mitsubishi Pajero. Of course, Grampi tried to talk me into an Alfa Romeo station wagon with leather seats but I would not be swayed. I knew what Fergus with his spew rug would do to leather seats. As a former used-car salesman in Adelaide he did, though, help me sell the Ford Laser, which he happily informed me for the first time was a 'hairdresser's car'. Now that I was selling it and had already married his daughter he could finally get that terrible burden off his chest. I objected to the Ford Laser being referred to as a hairdresser's car, until I realised that the only people ringing up to purchase it from the car sales ad were females, most of them hairdressers.

I was cashed up from the sale of the car and some money I had made on the stock market. My negotiations with the dealer from Mitsubishi are going well until he asks me what I do for a living. It is the first time I have been asked this question by someone who doesn't know me. I didn't think it would be so hard to answer yet almost immediately it sends me into a panic. I can't bring myself to tell him the truth. If I'm a super dad why is there this reluctance to unmask myself?

'I'm a journalist,' I say.

'Great, a journalist, and who do you work for?'

'Oh, I work from home.'

'So you're a freelance journalist.'

'Yeah, I'm a freelancer.'

'Which magazines do you write for?'

And on and one the questioning goes, rapid-fire, like he's shooting me with a rifle, because I'm not a freelance journalist and there are no magazines I'm writing for. All I do now is change nappies, clean up vomit and run around the house in my pyjamas. Then I start babbling away about trading shares like I'm some sort of day-trading financial genius getting myself further and further into trouble because there's no time to trade shares, there's no time for research, there's no time for anything. I can see his weight shifting forward as he leans into his desk because he's a car dealer, just like Grampi used to be, and is used to seeing through the bullshit, picking up on weakness.

Grampi has all sorts of stories from his days selling cars. He always said, 'Eddie LaPaglia was the best used-car salesman I ever saw. He always made his money in the buying.' I think Grampi also liked the story because Eddie LaPaglia was the father of actors Anthony and Jonathan LaPaglia and he would tell other stories about how they used to come over to their house in Adelaide and have dinner while the LaPaglia boys played billiards with Darlene and her brother Scott. I liked the story much better about how Grampi bought a car from a man and found out a few hours later that it didn't have a gear for reverse.

I bumble through the final part of the deal, angry at myself for not telling the truth. The dealer was about to make his money in the buying and the selling. What did I care what he thought anyway? I didn't even give him a chance to see what he thought. He nails me on the price and the add-ons: side rails, a roof rack, and a fabric protector for the seats. Darlene had watched all the macho negotiating with female curiosity. In the end she rescued me by directing the conversation in a different direction. On the way home she asks, 'Why didn't you tell him you were a stay-at-home dad?'

'I thought it would make me sound like a failure.'

'But you're not a failure,' she says.

'Why do I feel like a failure?' I asked.

'Well you're not.'

For my birthday not long afterwards Darlene buys me a deep-sea fishing trip off the Gold Coast. I'm hoping this gift will be better than the one for Father's Day, when I sat in a pair of disposable underpants in a steam room with another dad while we waited to be called out to be massaged; or the restaurant meal for our wedding anniversary, when the waiter spilled a tray of wine and beer on me and then gave me a shirt with 'drink at O'Tooles' as a replacement while they sent the other off to the dry-cleaners. Towards the end of the trip the skipper asks me what I do for a living. I brace myself for the stay-at-home-dad response while remembering too that the skipper has spent the better half of the day watching me spew over the back deck from the seasickness.

'I'm a stay-at-home dad,' I say, trying to maintain a steely resolve.

'Good on ya,' he says. 'I'd love to spend more time with my kids.'

Well that wasn't so hard, I think. The sun is shining directly into our eyes and the skipper is holding up his hand to shield it from the glare.

'But what do you *really* do?' he asks.

'Ummmmm . . . I'm a journalist,' I say.

'Oh, and who do you write for?'

★

109

I was a firm believer that I must be the one to get up at night for the baby in order for Darlene to get the rest she needed for work. She would be working twelve-hour days, coping with mountains of paperwork that she'd bring home in her briefcase. I thought it was a wonderful thing to say I would do this at barbecues to garner favour with the wives of my friends, although none of them, especially Sally, looked particularly impressed. In fact, they looked at me as if I had suddenly gone insane. My firm belief is quickly shelved within a few weeks of Darlene being back at work. Instead of getting up to Fergus when he woke screaming in the middle of the night I start poking her in the ribs in the hope that she will succumb to her maternal instincts. It is a dirty trick for a man will always outlast a woman when it comes to a crying baby. This leads to a rage in Darlene I have never encountered before, not even when the hormones where running wild during pregnancy, when one night as Fergus starts crying at about 4am I poke her in the ribs. She looms over me, a wild banshee armed with sharp fingernails, seething through clenched teeth.

'You poke me in the ribs again and I'll rip your nuts off. Now get up and see what's wrong with your son! You promised!' Perhaps now is not the right time to tell her about my new theory, my new firm belief, but I soldier ahead anyway. It goes something like this.

'In this new era of gender role reversal it should be you (the worker) that is helping me (the homemaker), not the other way around. If I was the one working then you would be the one poking me in the ribs begging for a reprieve just like Sally does with Andy, although she doesn't beg, she demands it. Not only is child rearing a physically demanding job with all the lifting and the bending and the nappy changing – it's estimated that stay-at-home mums lift almost one tonne per day as they care for their baby, which is probably why my biceps are getting bigger – but it also comes loaded with great mental demands: constantly scanning rooms like the Terminator to assess levels of risk, worrying about their development, their safety, whether they're eating all their food. And what about all the cleaning and cooking and shopping? I'm even in charge of all the birthday presents and cards for the nephews and nieces. Nobody told me how hard all that was going to be. The bottom line is that I'm fucking exhausted, consumed by tiredness that makes my head spin and my bones ache. I'm sick of getting up at the crack of dawn, of seeing the sun rise. The thought that the whole day is ahead of me without the chance for a rest until 7 or 8pm is almost too terrible to contemplate. I need more sleep. I need a thousand hours more.'

By now I suspect she would be feeling quite happy to be the one getting out of the house on a Monday. Work is a sanctuary from the madness of the week, when Fergus whirls around me like a spinning top. I say all these things in an attempt to secure more sleep. It is the act of a desperate man.

'You're a fucking lazy bastard,' she says getting out of bed. 'You're going to pay for this.'

A smile creeps across my face as she stomps off into Fergus's room to find out what is wrong. I would risk a thousand beatings for an extra hour's sleep.

Two words stick out like a neon sign on the routine sheet Darlene has left for me: 'Arsenic hour'. Just as the Bermuda Triangle strikes fear into the heart of weary mariners and aviators, so these words strike fear into the hearts of weary parents. In the early days before I was attuned to the moods of my child, I stumbled through the arsenic hour into dinner and bath time, emerging on the other side like a frightened traveller who has just emerged from a day lost in the scrub. The bewitching hour was 4pm, you could almost set your watch by it, when Fergus would hit the proverbial 'I'm tired out of my little baby mind' wall and start howling. At first I tried rocking him in my arms, playing with him, rattling toys in front of his eyes, singing songs, especially the Powderfinger songs he usually loved at other times of the day, but all it did was make him madder. In the end, just when I was about to ring Darlene up and tell her that 'even if we had to redraw the budget there is no way I can do this anymore', I stumbled onto the perfect antidote: a running pram.

It was my sister's, a streamlined three-wheeler with big fat go-anywhere tyres that you could run a marathon in with your child safely strapped inside. I didn't actually run with him in it, but we started taking long lovely walks through the eucalypt forests of the area, for the developers of the estate and another rival developer across the road had spent a small fortune on flat smooth walking tracks and sidewalks. As soon as the wheels hit the pavement Fergus calms down from his arsenic-hour attack and settles into the rhythm of the walk, the clicking of the tyres, the coolness of the afternoon, the singing of the birds. Soon I find these walks supremely addictive. I'm just as cranky as Fergus if for some reason we can't venture out. Not even rain can stop us as I buy a plastic cover sheet that clips onto the pram and means we can take on bad weather. Only lightning has the power to prevent us from our routine.

Soon we have become neighbourhood regulars, noticed by other mothers, especially a Chinese woman from down the road. I could spot her bow-legged walk from kilometres away. For a while she avoids me, lowering her head as I squeak past her. One day she stops, put her hands on her hips and says, 'You walk very far with that baby.' I was chuffed, thinking I was a good father; although later that night it occurs to me that maybe she was having a dig, maybe she was saying I was a bad father for walking so far with my baby. She never utters another word to me even though I saw her often.

The walks not only exercise my body but also my mind. I can feel myself coming to life as I pound along traversing huge hills that have me puffing for air at the top.

One day in the spring a magpie starts dive-bombing me halfway through my usual circuit. The magpie is angry and with good reason as day after day trees are being cut down to make way for new houses and new walking tracks. When I was at junior school a particularly nasty magpie would walk

up your back and peck you on the head if you made the mistake of throwing yourself on the ground to get away. It was
that vicious. One of the Christian Brothers shot it with an
air rifle and it must have clipped one of the magpie's wings
so it couldn't dive-bomb us anymore, but fluttered down in a
whirl of feathers like a helicopter, which wasn't nearly as scary.
I once wrote a story for the newspaper about a magpie that
had closed down a postal route due to its aggressive attacks.
I'd stood there with a notepad in my hand interviewing the
postie while the magpie dive-bombed us.

This magpie seems to have taken ownership of the entire
housing estate and sneaks up on me and . . . whoosh . . . fright-
ens me half to death. If I turn my back on him for a second he'll
have another go, and sits on branches in gum trees taunting me.
He's drawn blood and taken chunks out of my head but I'm not
going to let the magpie stop my arsenic-hour walks. Spring will
end and everything will get to normal. It's about this time that
I'm on the phone trying to organise Fergus's christening but I
am having trouble securing a church. The parish priest where I
used to attend is a nasty old bugger and is being very unhelpful
when I talk to him on the mobile. He is not the priest I knew
when I was growing up, who has long since passed away.

'Quite frankly, I'm tired of people like you wanting to get
married and have christenings here,' the grumpy priest says.
For a priest who is meant to be humble like Jesus and wash the
feet of the unclean I found his attitude quite disturbing.

'But Father, I went to church there for twenty years,' I say.
'My aunt has been going to church there for fifty years.'

'But you don't go now, do you?' he says.

It's at this point that the magpie comes down and takes a chunk out of the back of my head with its beak, drawing blood and knocking off my hat.

'Holy fuck,' I say, dropping the phone. The priest is not on the other end when I pick it up.

I wake one morning with a pain in my stomach that by midmorning has me doubled over in agony. Darlene is on a business trip to Melbourne for part of the week. Stuck out at Ipswich there is no one to help me and Fergus certainly does not care about my ailment. He wants his bottle, he wants his solids, he wants me to play with him, he wants his sleep, and he wants his afternoon walk at four o'clock. I struggle through the day and in the afternoon load him into the pram and complete the regular circuit, but my temperature is soaring as the fever grips me and the stabbing pain in my stomach intensifies. I want to curl up in the foetal position on the floor and moan, although there is still a bath to be had and dinner to prepare and the whole bedtime routine ahead of me. I'm about to learn that as the primary carer there are reserves of strength for such occasions. Who needs a trainer from *The Biggest Loser* to yell at you when you've got a baby that can do just as good a job?

I would never have thought it possible but when there is no one else to rely on and the safety and well being of your child is at stake you are capable of anything. I make it through the pain and collapse into bed, but the next day the pain has intensified. And now there is another whole day stretching before me. I struggle to the doctor with Fergus in tow. Before we had a baby I was hardly ever at the doctor, now I seem to be there every week. It's hard enough to piss in a bottle and poo in a jar at the best of times, let alone when you have a baby strapped to your chest, but that is what the doctor wants me to do. What must be going through Fergus's mind as he watches his father do his business in a bottle as I can't leave him in the surgery playpen unattended. I do, however, draw the line at dumping in the jar until I get home and can have some privacy.

In the end, after all their humiliating tests, they couldn't work out what was wrong with me. Another doctor gives me some antibiotics and the whole thing clears up overnight. Later, when I first take Fergus to childcare at three years of age the whole household gets sick. My immune system immediately buckles under the strain of a virus it hasn't seen since kindergarten in the seventies. Fergus was sick for just about half of his first year at childcare and each sickness he brought home knocked us down one by one. Once Darlene and I were both on the couch shivering with fever while he tore the house to pieces. Darlene's head swelled up and she broke out in a rash that covered her body from head to toe. My joints ached and my sheets were covered in sweat. Nanna had to come over and do the shopping for us. How would we have coped without the backup? How would a single parent have coped?

There are other days that I can scarcely believe I coped with either. Vicious colds and flus that would have kept me from work have to be ignored when you're the primary carer. Always in the back of my mind was the thought that a trip to the doctor for myself means organising babysitters and you have to use your babysitters wisely. One, because of the expense, and two, because you don't want to use up your babysitting credits with the grandparents, if you're lucky enough to have them, on something that involves pain and discomfort when you should be going out to dinner and a movie and reconnecting with your wife.

One morning I find bright red blood on the paper as I wipe myself. I ignore it for a while, as men are prone to do, hoping it will go away but soon the discomfort gets too much and I can't endure the razor blade-like pains anymore. I'm about to use one of my precious babysitting credits with Nanna and because of the embarrassing nature of my problem I tell her I need to leave her with Fergus because I'm having a 'business meeting'. She seems quite thrilled at the prospect that I might be returning to work. I know she probably feels quite ripped off with me being the main carer as she has been denied the opportunity to shop and have coffee with Darlene on a weekly basis as they wheel Fergus around Mount Ommaney Shopping Centre to buy baby clothes.

Before long I'm at the specialists' centre at South Brisbane, where I have a choice of lining up in one of several queues with little placards above the receptionists' desks. The people in the dermatology queue are here to have their moles checked. The people in the ophthalmology queue are here to have their eyes tested. The people in the colorectal queue are here to have the specialist shove something up their bum and peer into it with a flashlight. I can't bring myself to stand in the colorectal line as everyone in the waiting room will then know I have a problem with my bum. Instead, I pretend I have a problem with my eyes. The queue is a bit longer but that is a fair price to pay for avoiding the public gaze of ridicule. The pretty receptionist from the ophthalmology department must have encountered this problem before as she is still able to look up my appointment on her computer and confirm my arrival, which makes me wonder why they bother having signs up in the first place. She's very pleasant and professional but I know she's concealing a smirk in there somewhere.

Soon I'm prone on a bench holding a metal bar bolted to the wall as the colorectal surgeon with a name that sounds like an Italian pasta dish takes to me with something resembling a bicycle pump before injecting me with a needle so he can band the offending haemorrhoids. Haemorrhoids? By some sort of osmosis, had I, as a stay-at-home dad, started to acquire the ailments that were meant for women after childbirth? What other ailments did I have to look forward to? A leaking bladder? Incontinence pads? Anal fissures? You know you're in trouble when the doctor says, 'This might feel a little uncomfortable.' I figure at the very least it will be a good story to share with Andy and Nick and I can't help but think of Chevy Chase in the movie *Fletch* where he sings 'Moon River' during an unexpected digital examination and says, 'Ever done time, Doc?'

Out in the waiting room I'm forced to stand in the colorectal line to pay my bill and I don't care anymore because I've been violated and humiliated and the room starts spinning and I have to lie down on the chairs while another pretty receptionist gets me a glass of water.

'This happens all the time,' she says. I wait there for an hour till my head clears so I can get in the car and drive to pick Fergus up.

'How did your business meeting go?' Nanna asks expectantly.

'Wonderful,' I say.

I have an epiphany when I get home and it has nothing to do with what the doctor has done, or at least I hope not. That night after waddling around with Fergus through the afternoon routine and getting him to bed I finally understand the whole package, I understand what women have been going through all these years with all the cleaning and washing, battling through the sickness, putting their needs second to the needs of their child. I feel like shouting to women that I finally understand what it is all about, what all chauvinistic men choose not to understand, what my mother went through with four children while her husband went off to work.

I ring my mother and tell her I really appreciate what she did for us, saying, 'You were a great mum.' She seems quite chuffed.

'Maybe every man should do what you do,' she says. I feel like telling every mother I meet, old and young, single or married, 'I understand. I *really* understand.'

★

The game shifts up a notch when Fergus starts walking. You're so keen for them to walk and when they do you wish you'd been more patient. Life is so much easier when they aren't zooming around like Matchbox cars. First he starts cruising, where he'd move from one object to the next to support his weight. This is the stage where you have to move everything to higher ground as little hands start breaking anything they can grab. Then he is charging at me from across the room, yelping with delight as I scooped him into my arms. There is a price to pay for that freedom. The scope for accidents widens considerably. Stairs become a problem. Sharp edges on kitchen bench tops and coffee tables become a problem. They start falling over and whacking their heads. Those shrieks of delight when they first start walking soon turn to shrieks of pain as they land on their palms on the footpath for the first time. This is when the medicine cabinet with its Dorothy the Dinosaur Bandaids and the Savlon cream becomes your new best friend.

It all changes very quickly. I was learning that with children, just as you think you've got everything under control, the game changes and the whole routine has to be readjusted. Everything becomes so much harder and more dangerous when he starts climbing as well, looking for any signs of weakness in the fortress of the house. It isn't long before he works out how to open the front door, standing on tippy toes and flicking the lock. He is wearing me out before he started walking and now I realise I need more outside activities to entertain him or the already exhausting week could become too much. And then I see, in the local paper, an advertisement for Kinda Gym.

Up until now I have led a rather sheltered existence, stuck out at Ipswich, feeding and walking and playing with my baby. I was so busy I didn't even consider adding anything extra to my workload. And this will be the first time I will come face to face with mothers. The Kinda Gym teacher moves about with enthusiasm and energy and soon Fergus is walking across balance beams and running about kicking coloured balls and hanging off rings. There is a mother who has a toddler at Kinda Gym and two more strapped to her front and back. She has legs like tree trucks and is sweating from the exertion. Everything is going well until Fergus tumbles into the pit filled with foam that the gymnasts use to perfect their somersaults. I lift Fergus out but am overcome with an enthusiasm to jump into the foam too, sinking in it up to my neck. It's like I'm struggling in quicksand and I have to call the instructor over to help me out.

Perhaps I am paranoid but I sense at Kinda Gym, as they sit around singing songs about rainbows and cleaning up – 'Clean up clean up everybody everywhere clean up clean up everybody do your share' – that the women do not want me there. They have got no makeup on; their hair is a mess. Is this why nobody will look me in the eye, return my smile? It's almost as though I don't exist, that I am the invisible man. It is the same when I go to swimming lessons. The last thing the women about me want to be seen in is their swimming costumes and I struggle to make conversation with them. In the nappy change room there is a noticeable silence when I enter with Fergus. Whatever conversation the mothers were having will have to wait until I have left the area. During a lesson I go to help one mother out of the pool when she slips at the edge and see that her pubic hair is stretching out of her togs, almost to her knees. *Wow*, I think to myself, and I thought I'd let myself go. Now I know why *she* didn't particularly like having a man in her class.

I'm with Fergus at our local park. This is another area where women will not look at me. They stand in groups chatting amongst themselves. Because I have a child with me I am not considered a threat but breaking into those tight circles they cluster in seems impossible. At the park there are monkey bars, a jungle gym with a slide and a tall tower of climbing ropes that reminds me of the Eiffel Tower. Running down one perimeter is the jewel in the crown: the flying fox. It occurs to me that there are no wooden seesaws in parks anymore and perhaps that's a good thing. We used to use them as catapults. One of the neighbourhood kids must have flown twenty metres when my brothers and I all rushed to the other end and sent him hurtling through the air. His left arm hung limp at his side afterwards and we told him he was a wimp if he cried and that he must not breathe a word of his injury, especially how he got it, to anyone. Later we found out he had broken his collarbone. He'd also sung like a canary: his mum rang our mum, and we were sent to bed early after dinner without any ice-cream.

Also missing is the whirligig – a spinning wheel with the metal bars that you clung to for dear life as G-forces that would have scared a jet fighter pilot threatened to rip the skin off your face. It would spit dizzy children out at breathtaking speeds. The adults who had drunk too much beer and wine at barbecues or kids parties would always succumb to the temptations of the whirligig and would be spat out too. I remember a parent falling off the whirligig at Andy's grade-five party and hearing his back crack. The seesaw and the whirligig are long gone now, banned by councils worried about insurance claims. If they are so worried about getting sued why are they making tall towers out of ropes where a child can climb up into the sky and tumble down just as quickly, which Fergus has done a few minutes previously? He's still too little to get very high off the ground so I wasn't too worried. He came running over to me wailing and I dusted him off but now he's back on it again trying to climb even higher. Should I stop him? Is that what being a good parent is all about? How is he meant to learn about life if I hold his hand every step of the way? I'm praying he won't fall again but he gives up and wants to go on the swings. I push him back and forth as he urges me to go faster and higher. He is squealing with pleasure.

'Yeahhhhhh,' he screams as his hat falls off and lands on the soft, spongy ground.

There's a kid's party starting up near the park benches and the barbecues. Children are running about in shiny pointed hats, blowing whistles. The noise is getting louder and louder as more guests arrive. A Subaru station wagon pulls up in the car park and out pops a father dressed in a Scooby Doo outfit. It's late afternoon although it's still hot outside, well above thirty degrees Celsius, and the man in the outfit is helping his wife get all the stuff out of the back of the car – chairs, a picnic basket, an esky full of drinks and ice blocks. The children at the party are thrilled at his arrival and flock about him, rubbing their hands on his furry outfit like they are patting a dog. His daughter looks thrilled. Her daddy is the best daddy in the world. All the other kids are jealous as he dances around.

There is another man beside me on the swings. He is pushing his child higher and higher, just like I am with Fergus.

'That prick dressed up as Scooby Doo is making us all look bad,' he says.

The isolation of staying at home with Fergus might be testing the lines of communication with my wife but the bond with my son is blossoming. It is so strong that it brings Darlene to tears. They are not tears of joy. We are out at Andy's place and Fergus will not go to her when he falls over. He struggles out of her grip and reaches out for me.

'Dadda!' I see the awkward looks Sally and Andy give each other. In the silence that follows I can almost hear Darlene's heart shattering.

7

KNOCKING ON DOORS

My father is dying of cancer. His pancreas is riddled with the disease. Some of the cancer has broken off and travelled through his blood to other parts of his body, mainly his liver. The doctor who opened him up told him he has six months to live.

'Soon you'll get your wish and I'll be dead,' my father says coolly to me over the phone. It is exactly the sort of thing my father excels at: emotional blackmail. It is why I have avoided him all these years. And now, unbelievably, I can sense my father's almost maniacal delight in having one last mighty trump card to play, an ace in the deck, the one that he can use to win the game of 'how much do you love me'?

I have not spoken to my father for nearly two years. Not since I discovered that he'd cheated on my mother. My father tried to make a joke of it when I confronted him about the infidelities, like he always did when it came time to face the consequences of his actions. He might have blasted my mother and my siblings regularly with his anger, with his threats of violence, but humour was his other weapon of choice, the antidote to the dark moods that swept the house. Fear and laughter were regular bedfellows under our roof, like living with Freddy Krueger and Benny Hill. After his bad moods he'd always become rather placid, funny and charming, the mask he showed to the world, which is why no one ever believed what a monster he was at home. One moment he'd be screaming obscenities, slamming doors, standing at the dinner table with an axe he'd got from under the house, vowing to kill us all; the next we'd be sitting in front of the television laughing with him as he guffawed at Paul Hogan or the famous Irish comedian Dave Allen.

'You know, Ben, don't be so quick to judge me,' Dad said of the affairs. 'In France it is common for the man of the house to take on a mistress.' He said it so convincingly and without a hint of remorse that I was almost taken in, I almost believed him that I was the one with the problem.

'I can't remember the last time I saw you wearing a beret,' I replied coldly before breaking off all contact.

And, now, here he is on the phone all these years later, congratulating me on the birth of Fergus, who he is yet to meet, while also telling me in a calm and measured voice that his time on the planet is almost over. My head is spinning. My only fear as I had walked towards the phone to answer it a few minutes earlier was that maybe it would be a telemarketer wanting to sell me a holiday or a new electricity account.

Fergus's birth had signified a new beginning for me, a fresh start to my distorted view of fatherhood, of redemption even. Everything I'd been doing with Fergus had been measured against what *he* could never provide me as a father: patience, stability and unconditional love. Every time Fergus spilled drinks on the table, dropped food on the couch, drew long colourful marks with crayon on the white walls, left poo in the hallway, peed on the floorboards, picked up the remote control and hurled it across the room, I took a deep breath and centred myself. *I will not be like him.* I gauged my success as a father on my ability to remain calm when disaster struck or tension levels rose. *I can control myself.* When Fergus threw himself on the ground and had a tantrum because he didn't want to brush his teeth: *I will not get angry.*

This didn't mean I was a pushover. When Fergus was old enough to know the difference between right and wrong he would get a warning when he behaved badly: 'Please don't stand on the chair, chairs are for sitting. If you stand on the chair again I'll have to put you in the naughty corner.' If he did it again I'd place him in the designated spot – one minute for every year of his life. When I started to do this there was a battle of wills. He would leave the corner and I would place him back there – out and in, out and in – careful not to get into an argument with him as per the Supernanny's advice. At first his reluctance to sit in the corner could go on for up to an hour, just like it had when I was trying to get him to stay in his cot of an evening. When I finally got him to stay in the naughty corner for the required time he began to say the most horrible things when I returned: 'I hate you. I wish Mummy was here, not you.' But once he hung his head in shame and apologised for the bad things he'd said. Then, amazingly, he told me how much he loved me. *You see, Dad, I'm better than you. I'm setting boundaries. My child will love me more than I love you.*

Of course, this mask of control I was putting on for my child was a bluff. Sooner or later the mask was going to be pulled off and the man behind it would be revealed, whoever he was. My calm demeanour was like a duck paddling across a lake, effortless on the surface, all spinning and churning below. But I didn't know that then, did I?

I consider hanging up on him. This is all too difficult, just like it always is with him. There is a long pause. Finally, I do what I always do. For the sake of whatever family unity remains I agree to keep the peace.

'Okay, Dad, what about we catch up for a coffee?' I say. But it feels surreal this time because the stakes are so high. He's dying and I'm only speaking to him on the condition that he gets on with the business of dying: *Don't you go fucking this up by getting better!*

I read once that children worship their parents until they're eight years old, learn from them up till twelve, and question them up till they're eighteen. After that they pretty much assume their parents are idiots until one day they have children of their own. It's only then they finally understand and appreciate the true perils of parenting. To a certain extent I'd found this to be true. When I moved out of home in my early twenties to do my cadetship at the newspaper I'd stopped asking my parents for anything. I guess I assumed they were idiots. My mother's advice grated on me: 'Are you eating well?' 'Do you have enough warm clothes?' She worried incessantly if I ever made the mistake of telling her I was unwell: 'When are you going to visit the doctor?' And I would sooner subscribe to the ranting of Charles Manson than subject myself to my father's advice. My life was about being everything he wasn't and I think he suspected this and it made him angry. Why else did he keep reminding me of how much I owed him?

When I did see my parents after I left home all we did was argue. For the life of me I couldn't imagine how any of this would change when I was married and a few little ones appeared on the scene. But it had, or at least it had with my mother. After two years at home with Fergus I understood how terrible it must have been for Mum, stuck at home with four kids in a loveless marriage, the drawn-out days of isolation when he'd work long hours and play golf and cricket on the weekends. Did she know about the affairs, too? Like most women she probably suspected.

Mum was an only child and had no family to turn to in Brisbane. Her mother, an energetic outspoken woman by all accounts, whom I have only seen in photographs, died of bowel cancer not long after my sister was born. Mum often told me things would have been different if her mother had lived longer. She wouldn't have put up with the way Dad treated her daughter. She would have given him a real tongue-lashing.

Mum's father, a solicitor, lived a two-hour drive away in Toowoomba on the rural Darling Downs. Grandad was a man of few words, from a different generation, raised in the Depression when you didn't complain but got on with things. When his wife was diagnosed with the cancer the oncologist had told him, as the man of the house, about the terminal nature of the illness before he told her – that's how much times have changed as a doctor today would tell the patient first, as it should be. I was still in primary school when Grandad died of a heart attack. He was about to take a shower and they found him in the bathroom after he didn't turn up for work. My art teacher took me outside and told me that there was bad news. Grandad was dead, and my mum was coming to get me. I cried and she put her arms around me.

'There, there,' she said. 'Let it all out.' That was the first time I realised how quickly life could change, how you could be in art class one minute and outside crying in the car park getting hugged by your art teacher, who smelled like perfume and watercolours, the next. I loved Grandad and I knew you cried when people you loved died, just like I cried when Jackson, our pet Labrador, died when the vet came over and injected him with the needle that Dad called the 'green dream'. As I waited for Mum I started remembering things about Grandad, how he'd pour Schweppes lemonade into colourful metal cups he kept in the fridge. Sometimes he'd give me warm Cadbury Dairy Milk chocolate that he had pulled out of the cupboard and broken apart with his arthritic fingers.

'You've been a good boy, have some of this too.' The bubbles in the lemonade fizzed against the chocolate when I mixed them together in my mouth. And how, whenever we visited Grandad, he could never find the key to the piano in his lounge room, or the 'drawing room' as he called it. Of course, he knew we would just bash away at the keys, make too much noise, and put the whole thing out of tune.

'Now, where did I put that key? Dear me, it's disappeared again. Maybe next time,' he always said. I never got to play that piano, not once. He smoked Capstan cigarettes in a blue-and-white packet and loved Arnott's Shredded Wheatmeals smothered with butter, which he nibbled on while he drank his Bushells tea. He used old-fashioned English sayings like, 'By Jove, it's a smashing day'. Once at Easter he shuffled down the hallway late at night in his slippers to brush his teeth and I sat there shaking with nerves in my room thinking the brushing sound was the Easter bunny eating the carrots I'd left outside my door.

When Grandad died, I drove with Mum and Dad up the range to Toowoomba for the funeral. From memory I was the only child in the car, suitably attired in my dress school uniform with a tie, dark blue jacket, tailored shorts and long socks. Dad screamed at Mum the whole way, flying into one of his rages on the two-hour journey as she sobbed in the front seat.

'Stop it,' she pleaded. 'Not today. Not now.' I can't remember why he was angry with her but the thought popped into my mind that, whatever complexities of the adult world, my father was evil and you didn't yell at people when they were going to funerals. I wished then that we were going to his funeral instead. I wished he was the one that was dead. I stared out the window and watched the cows in the paddocks and the long lines of crops stretching out towards the horizon before the car started climbing up the winding range. I imagined I was outside, looking down on the world from the clouds, like an angel, far away from the car and all the yelling.

After the funeral we stopped at a real estate agency so Dad could get an appraisal on Grandad's house. Mum sat in the car sobbing, her red eyes hidden behind her huge sunglasses, the ones that were popular at the time.

'There, there. Let it all out,' I said.

Mum always told me when I was growing up to have as many children as possible when I got married, to breed like a rabbit: 'You don't want to impose the loneliness of being an only child on anyone.' She had strong reasons for this advice, of course. It seemed incredible to me that Mum had no relatives to turn to when she was upset. I had lots of cousins and aunts and uncles because Dad came from a large family. At Christmas time it took up the whole day just visiting them. Mum's mother had been an only child. Grandad's only sister was a spinster and she was long gone. When Grandad died she also lost her great protector, a role filled in later years by my older brother.

Before the divorce, Mum seemed to have resigned herself to fate, thinking escape was impossible. When Mum had a hysterectomy Dad had told her that he hoped she died right there on the operating table: ''cause that's what you deserve for ruining my life, you heartless bitch!' I wondered why, if she hated him so much, she had gone on a nice holiday to South Africa and Kenya with Dad when they got the money from Grandad's estate, which by now had been long spent. But instead of enjoying her retirement Mum talked often about Dad striding around the house in a rage, threatening to kill her while dressed only in underpants – no doubt the gigantic Y-fronts that men seem to favour in old age. I found it hard not to sink into a depression after hearing these stories. I wanted to live my own life now. I did not want to think about my father standing there in a rage in large white undies.

One day, after another round of complaining, we had an intervention of sorts. All of us kids told Mum that she wasn't going to live with Dad anymore. She could stay with my sister until the separation was worked out.

'It's time to take action,' my younger brother said.

'You must return me this instant,' she cried out. But then she calmed down and took a few deep breaths. 'Okay, you're right. It's time for this to end.'

Dad thought she'd come to her senses and come back to him, like she always did. He taunted her. He mocked her. She held firm. The divorce proceeded and he moved out to his luxury apartment at New Farm. Gradually his children drifted away from him. From time to time one of us would make up with him but once you were back on his radar it wouldn't be long before he would target you again for some minor indiscretion. His concept of the father–son bond involved me bowing and scraping and telling him how grateful I was for everything he'd given me. 'You'd never be anything without me,' he'd say.

After hearing about the cancer I ask Mum for her advice about whether or not I should reconnect with Dad. Mum has been so helpful to me since Fergus was born. Sometimes she has driven out to Ipswich to look after Fergus when I've been sick, fixing meals, washing and ironing clothes.

'You must do the right thing,' she says. 'If not for him, for me. People will think that I made you turn against your father. He'll be dead soon and then we can all move on.'

I take Fergus with me to my father's apartment in New Farm. It is a Monday morning just after breakfast. Over my shoulder I have a nappy bag filled with snacks, towels and bottles. My father opens the door and looks tanned and well, meaty around his jowls. He has a big pot belly. He does not look like a man about to die. The thought crosses my mind that he's playing a trick on me . . . *Perhaps he's not dying after all* . . . a thought that then sparks a guilty conscience for even Dad, with all his faults and his brilliant mind games, would not be capable of such a thing. Dad is dressed in a light blue business shirt with white cuffs and a collar and dark blue slacks. He is wearing comfortable black shoes. I can sense that my father wants to hug me. *Welcome back into the fold, my son!* Powerful emotions swim in my head and I wonder what he would think if he knew that deep down, at that moment, I would prefer to headbutt him, punch him in the nose, smother him with a pillow, get the whole awful business of dying over and done with quickly. I settle for a handshake, keeping a respectable distance, standing my ground.

'Look at this handsome guy,' Dad says, ruffling Fergus's hair. 'What a little champion!'

Fergus smiles back, his few teeth sticking through his gums, but I can feel his grip tightening on me as he looks at this stranger.

'This is your Grandpa,' I tell him.

'Ferger Burger,' Dad calls him, tickling him under the chin. I can tell he wants to hold him but I'm reluctant to let Fergus go. He is my son after all and it's me who is calling the shots here. It annoys me that I feel the need to apologise to Dad for not seeing Fergus but the truth is that if he'd rung and wanted to see him I wouldn't have stopped him, I wouldn't have said no. Whatever the reasons for my dislike of my father I would never deny Fergus the chance to know his grandfather. I knew that Dad would be pleasant and amusing company for Fergus, that he would be a terrific grandfather, for he would never show his true side to him. But he's never rung, has he? Perhaps he prefers it this way because I know he has been going around Brisbane telling his friends that I wouldn't let him see his new grandson. Perhaps he likes being an object of pity, because pity can get you enormous amounts of attention and Dad loves attention.

Pity is a very powerful weapon for someone with a clever manipulative mind. It got him invited to my wedding.

'How can you not invite your own father,' he'd said when I made the threat. When he sensed that wasn't swaying me he worked on Darlene's parents, until they insisted I invite him to keep the peace.

'What harm can he do?' they said. But at the wedding Dad got up and made a speech that went on for half an hour when he was meant to talk for only a minute. He talked about all his kids, except me. He thanked everyone for coming when it was Nanna and Grampi who were paying for everything. Grampi was standing in the background and I heard him say to his mates, 'Can you believe this guy?' His friends started to move forward towards the lectern and it looked like it was about to get ugly but luckily Dad sat down. My niece, who'd been a flower girl, had been sitting on my lap during this time and she asked me, 'Why are you so sad, Uncle Ben?' That question then crossed my mind, 'What harm can he do?'

I walk inside his apartment, which overlooks the Story Bridge and the loop of the river at Kangaroo Point. It is a magnificent view but the unit smells mouldy and the carpet hasn't been vacuumed properly. There are wine stains under the bits of food on the floor around the coffee table. Later when I get a glass from the cupboard it's dirty and the fridge is empty save for a few takeaway food containers scattered about the shelves. He's living the bachelor lifestyle. Since Mum stopped looking after him he has obviously struggled with the basics. The apartment has a laundry attached to the kitchen and I can see that there is a load of washing inside, wet and soggy, and needing to be hung up. It's hard not to feel sorry for him and he is obviously trying hard to be friendly to me, using all the old tricks, lots of compliments, oozing charm.

It would be nice to erase all the pain of the past thirty-odd years and start again, but that is not going to happen, not in a few minutes. That was what Dad was expecting and he can't understand why no one else wants to play happy families when he decides to start smelling the roses again. For the moment we can only work with what is new and fresh, and not corrupted, and all we have that is new is Fergus, my son, which annoys me. I finally take Fergus off my hip and put him down on the floor. Like a wind-up toy waiting to be unleashed, he zeros in on a putter lying on the carpet and begins bashing golf balls about the apartment, swatting at them with hockey-like swings as the club is too big for him. One of the balls rockets across the floor and cracks like a bullet into the glass coffee table in the living room. *Crash!* It's an impressive shot from a toddler.

'No problem, no problem at all,' Dad says, walking over and examining the damage, and I could tell he meant it. Dad never seemed to stress about some kind of stuff, but others . . . Once I left the handbrake off Mum's yellow Volvo station wagon and it ran down the backyard into a gum tree. When he came home from work he barely uttered a word about it, just shook his head and laughed . . . *you bloody idiot* . . . before retreating into his cave. There had been no punishment, no grounding. It seemed like such an anti-climax because my stomach had been churning all day as I had waited for him to appear: *Wait till your father comes home!* I knew I deserved to be punished. In fact, I wanted to be punished, but life continued on as normal. The following evening, though, he discovered purple flowers from the jacaranda tree in the pool, which was my responsibility to clean. For that he tried to hit me, pulling me out of my chair and throwing wild telegraphed punches at my head. He smelt of the dental surgery, stale and sterile. But he hadn't reckoned on my size. When I finally subdued him and held him against the wall by the shoulders he was puffing and panting and bits of spittle had settled around the edges of his mouth.

He felt brittle and weak under my grip, more like papier-mâché than flesh and muscle. There was almost nothing to him, and that night I had worried that he was a hollow man without a soul. Our relationship changed after that for he must have felt the shift in strength. He never came at me with his fists again. He came at me with his toxic tongue, though, trying to turn the tables on me with his spite: *You'll never be anything in this life! You're a fucking parasite.* But his inconsistencies to punishment led to a unique kind of tension in the house. His rules, if there were any, were impossible to understand. You never knew how he'd react. All of us kids had weaknesses that he preyed upon. He invited you in with an understanding, 'Tell me about your problems,' and then when the moment took him he would hurl back your insecurities.

★

'He seems to have some athletic ability,' my father says, referring to Fergus's golf shot. 'Perhaps he's the next Tiger Woods.' It is meant to be an icebreaker but in my eyes it is far from it. I know from reading magazines that Tiger Woods' father used to jangle keys in Tiger's ears on the practice tee before he hit golf shots, to help him focus. At night he made him listen to subliminal tapes: *You will be a champion. You will be the best.* My father had a very different approach. He would yell at me on the way home from athletic contests if I didn't win. His face would go beetroot red, spittle flying on the steering wheel of his green Jaguar sedan with the cream leather seats as we drove home from running carnivals or rugby games. Sometimes he would hide in the car park, even behind trees, and watch me train before he picked me up.

'You're not trying hard enough! Did you think you could fool me?' Once I threw an intercept pass and lost the game in an under-twelves match and he yelled at me for an hour straight, from the outer northern suburbs where the game was played to Indooroopilly in the west. I stared out the car window and zoned out, imagining I lived in a home where there was no yelling and where fathers didn't throw chairs through windows or tins of coffee into ceiling fans when they came home in bad moods, especially bad moods caused by me because I didn't win. He videotaped everything with a camera attached to a bulky black and silver recorder, one of the first video cameras on the market, and then he would watch and analyse the tapes when he got home on the even bulkier Philips colour television – over and over again. When there were no school athletics carnivals for me to run in Dad would drive around Brisbane and look for others I could enter, like I was some sort of prize pony. Other parents thought he was the perfect father. Other children whose parents never went to a game or dropped off their kids at the running track thought I was the luckiest kid in the world.

I was a state champion runner and a winger in the Queensland Junior Rugby Union team, but some nights I wished that God had never given me any talent. Being fast was a curse. I envied those kids who seemed to enjoy sport; how they could still laugh when they lost. I wondered if their fathers yelled at them when they got in the car to go home. Andy said he'd never heard his dad raise his voice: 'My dad is boring. Your dad is so funny.' I never raised the subject again after that. I knew there was something wrong with my father, the way he watched those videotapes over and over, and felt there was something wrong within my family with all the wrong kind of laughing and the crying, but I would keep this to myself.

I could never understand how Dad could be charming to outsiders, like the staff where we picked up our Chinese take-aways, yet moments later in the car his smile would vanish from his face and be replaced by a listless stare. Whenever we went out to dinner he'd have the waitresses falling over themselves to please him but on the way home he'd start roaring at Mum for some infraction, like she hadn't laughed at one of his jokes or hadn't been supportive enough and had embarrassed him with her silence.

'What sort of wife are you?' Dad would shout. When he was on a roll he'd scroll through a list of offences she'd caused him from all the way back in the fifties when they met right through to the present. When he was really angry he'd get stuck into her parents, always saying that Granddad was tight with his money.

Sometimes on holidays at the Sunshine Coast he would take me to various surf lifesaving clubs and enter me in races against local nippers in the beach sprints. In the mornings Dad would mark out a running track on the sand near the groin that had been built beside the mouth of the river and I'd race to it, down the main beach at Noosa. He wanted me to win an Australian title and he would have me sprinting for an hour up and down sandhills until I threw up.

'You're weak,' Dad would say, staring at the vomit. 'You've got to toughen up.' But back then I loved him. I loved him more than anything in the world, and I would do anything to please him. All the abuse was worth enduring for just a few minutes of basking under the warm glow of praise when he'd buy me fizzy drinks, packets of chicken Twisties, and pat me on the head.

'You're a champion,' he'd say. 'You're a winner.'

I would pray to God to make Dad not be in a bad mood. I would pray to God to make me fast and perfect, to give me wings so I never lost a race or threw an intercept pass. Perhaps that's why I'm standing here in his apartment, pretending that everything is normal, and we're father and son catching up on the good old days. There can be no other reason. I want to please him one more time, to pretend for a fleeting moment that our relationship is healthy and normal. I want him to tell me that I'm a good father, a great father.

It annoys me that I still love him.

A few weeks later and Fergus and I are back at my father's apartment. Dad is heavily medicated. The drugs seem to have a soothing impact on his personality, ironing out the anger. It makes me wonder what sort of father he would have been if he'd been able to control himself when the dark moods took him away from us. I found myself telling him what he'd said back then when he was angry and he'd say, 'I never said that, you're making it up.' A few times in our conversations the subject strayed to Mum. Normally her name would be enough to set him off but I never saw him flinch. Once, before the divorce, when Dad was at his worst, Mum had slipped Valium into his food, grinding up the drugs into a powder first and sprinkling it into his spaghetti bolognaise. I had had another method of revenge after he yelled at me one time too often. I went down to the soccer oval near our house and gathered green ants in a jar and sprinkled them under the sheets in his bed in the study where he slept. His cave was cold as he ran the air conditioner day and night. Before I went to sleep that night I made extra sure the French doors to my room on the verandah were locked from the inside. Later I heard him howl with pain when one of the greenies got him.

★

Mum hires nurses from a palliative care agency. Like all of us, she is determined to do her bit, and he wants to die in his unit overlooking the river. The nurses work in shifts around the clock, giving him his pain-relieving medicine, shaving his face, helping him dress and take showers. They will be there until he dies. He has lost a lot of weight now and the pot belly is gone. Almost overnight the illness seems to have gripped him, sunk its teeth into living flesh. Death is stalking him, waiting to take him away. The arrival of more nurses confirms this and they hover around, attending to his every whim, waiting for the inevitable. It makes me wonder what might have happened if he hadn't been independently wealthy. The burden might have been placed on us, his children. His money gives us space to come and go as we please rather than act as carers, and we are able to maintain a certain emotional distance.

The physical evidence of his impending demise might be compelling but the fact that Dad is dying still seems impossible to me. Every time the thought of his death comes into my head I brush it away into a corner to be dealt with later. This is not because I don't want him to die but because I keep telling myself that it doesn't mean anything to me if he does, which is really a far more frightening concept for I wonder what sort of person that makes me, what sort of emotionless monster I am becoming. More than anything I don't want to be like him. More than anything it terrifies me that I *will* be like him and I don't have any say in the matter, as if our shared DNA will mutate and like the Hulk I won't be able to control the anger.

I used to think I was angry because of all the tiredness from raising children, with all the sleepless nights and all the work that comes from being a stay-at-home dad. I thought I was angry when I should have been happy. But now I know I was just scared. That acting angry was just a front for being scared. And I was tired of being scared.

Dad still has the strength to pick Fergus up, tickling his tummy with his forehead.

'Hi, I'm Grandpa Col,' he says. His tickling Fergus's tummy with his forehead is the same thing I do with my son, and the fact that the gesture is so eerily similar unnerves me. I'm thinking to myself about that old saying: the apple doesn't fall far from the tree. We sit down in his comfy leather couch while Fergus roams the room looking for something to break. Dad seems happy to talk about his latest business venture. He is pumping vast sums of money, he tells me, into a gold factory in Shenzhen City in the southern part of China near Hong Kong. China is emerging as an economic power and, even though he's dying, Dad is determined to be part of the excitement.

'The sleeping dragon has been awakened,' he says.

'But you're a dentist, Dad, what do you know about gold jewellery?'

'I have a business manager taking care of that – an expert.' I am happy to let my father talk about his dreams of world domination through the gold jewellery business in China for it means we don't have to broach any of the subjects that we should really be talking about; about how he ruined my child-hood, the yelling, the fear, why he cheated on Mum, why he failed all of us. Once, when it got really bad at home, I packed a small bag and tried to run away, sleeping in my neighbours' tree house high up off the ground. It was cold and the mosqui-toes were bad. I'd start getting hungry and soon I grew tired of running away. I'd sneak back through my window and unpack my backpack, sometimes hoping that Dad and Mum would be there worrying about me, but they never were, they hadn't even known I had gone.

This memory makes me wonder about the street kids you see in the Queen Street Mall and the kinds of lives they are escaping from. How bad do they have it to push through with their determination to run away? I'd never made it further than the neighbours' yard but they were roughing it under cardboard boxes and newspaper. Perhaps my father is right. Perhaps I am weak.

Before I leave the nurse takes me aside.

'You're father is so funny,' she says. 'You must have laughed a lot when you were growing up.'

'Yeah, it was a riot,' I say, trying to hide the sarcasm. I'm reminded of my dad sitting at the breakfast table by him-self eating his cornflakes, before picking up his briefcase and heading off to work where he would tell jokes to his patients while drilling into their gums and polishing their teeth.

My father once gave me a present of a charcoal drawing of Tea Tree Bay on the Sunshine Coast. He had had it framed. It was there, when I was little, that he had carried me on his shoulders a few hundred metres along the winding path around the headland in the Noosa National Park, through the pandanus palms, across the boulders and onto the sand at the bay. Before I scooted off to play in the rock pools with my siblings Dad would dig a deep hole, explaining to me the importance of a solid base, scooping out the cool wet sand till he was reaching in up to his armpit. Then, and only then, would he insert the wooden handle of the umbrella, filling in around it and packing it down with the sand he'd just dug out. Up the umbrella would go, nice and secure and blocking out the harsh sunlight. Mum would fold out a chair under it and take out a book to read. Dad would put on his terry towelling hat and zinc on his nose. Dad gave me that picture of Tea Tree Bay because he wanted me to remember the days when I worshipped him, when I thought he was a superhero. But I couldn't stand looking at it when I took it home. I stared at the charcoal lines and could feel the emotions it conjured up. I tried to like it, to love it even. I hung it on the wall in my study. After a week I took it down and gave it to St Vincent de Paul.

Dad continues to talk about China. He tells me that the manager of his gold factory, a Chinaman nicknamed 'Big Sam', burst into tears when he told the workers of his illness. Dad had lived in China for a while before he came back to battle his illness, and I still find it hard to visualise a suburban dentist managing to set up a gold factory in China. Dad was anything but predictable. Big Sam might have been upset enough to cry but I'm not. Big

Sam didn't live with my father. Big Sam wouldn't have lasted two seconds in my house with his lack of speed and his tears.

Then Dad ushers Fergus and me downstairs to show off his new Mercedes-Benz sports car.

'It cost me a quarter of a million dollars,' he says proudly. 'I always wanted a car like this, but your mother wouldn't let me.' It is indeed a stunning machine, sleek and silver, and even with my limited knowledge of cars I know the AMG badge on the rear of the two-door coupe means that it is an elite performance car.

'She's a beauty,' I say, opening up the bonnet and running my hand over the supercharged V8 engine. What I really want to say is: *Do you know I could pay my mortgage off with that sort of money?* But there was no point in even thinking that as Dad has already made it clear to me that none of us will be getting any of his money when he dies.

'You all abandoned me long ago and I've made other arrangements.' He again makes the point very clear, which doesn't surprise me because Dad loves talking about money. He particularly loves speculating about how much money other people have and if he has more than them.

'I'm not here for the money,' I tell him.

'Just so you know,' Dad says.

Standing in the garage and looking at his expensive sports car, the ridiculousness of the situation overwhelms me. *What am I here for?* To play the dutiful son? To give my father the Hollywood horseshit ending he wants, with us all sitting around his bedside singing 'Kumbaya' as he withers away and drifts off to greener pastures? Does he deserve that kind of ending? And what sort of person am I for even thinking like this? For all his faults, Dad was a good provider: we never starved, we lived in a nice house, went to good schools, were taken on expensive holidays. Materially we were given every advantage. It could have been so much worse. What if he'd been abusive *and* a bad provider? The bottom line was that if we needed anything materially Dad would have given it to us.

'I love you so much I'd give you my bone marrow if you were sick,' he liked to say, and I knew he meant it. That was where it got confusing. If he loved me enough to give me his bone marrow why did I feel that he'd never loved *me*? All the talk of money and materialism, of thinking about bone marrow, is making me angry again, confused and angry. *This is not what this is all about.* Here I am again going over the same ground expecting a different answer, the very definition of insanity. The muscles in my neck start to stiffen as I grind my teeth. I worry that the negative vibes will rub off on Fergus, who is happily perched on my shoulders. I worry that I will turn out like my father and Fergus will hate me.

'Perhaps you could take a photo of me and Fergus in front of the car,' Dad says.

I know what he is playing at. He wants a photo that will confirm to Fergus in years to come what a big shot he was, leaning on the bonnet of some stupid Mercedes for all eternity. It's not going to happen. He's not going to use my son as a pawn in his little power game.

'I think it's time we got going,' I say.

8

FINDING THE MIDDLE GROUND

Amid all the talk of death there is the joy of new life. Darlene is pregnant again. Much to my mother's delight Fergus will have a sibling to play with. He will not be an only child. I hadn't imagined that making a second baby would be so easy, especially when the first time had been so difficult. But it was. Darlene was much more prepared with charts and ovulation times, temperatures and spreadsheets; there were days during the month when it was red hot like a not-to-be-missed sale at the shops, and days when it really wasn't worth the effort. I liked the first time around much more, when every day was like a great sale. We'd only been trying for a month when Darlene emerged from the bathroom and we watched together as the little cross on the panel turned blue.

But it is tough watching the pregnancy progress, and not just because my father was dying at the same time. We also carry with us fears of miscarriage and, as her belly grows and her ankles swell and her moods fluctuate, I find I just can't give her the attention she deserves. I have Fergus to care for now as well, and he craves my attention. My duties as a stay-at-home dad mean my energies have to be directed in two directions: Fergus during the day and Darlene at night. I soon find that, like most men, I am not very good at multi-tasking. Fergus gets everything. And then the times I do have free I think about my dad. The fuel tank has run dry. There is nothing left for Darlene.

As Darlene gets bigger and bigger the pace at work starts to grind her down too. Watching her get into the car of a morning and strap the seat belt around her belly makes me uneasy, as if I've failed my wife by not protecting and providing for her, none of which I seem capable of anymore. The Catholic guilt begins to work its magic. I am a failure in the eyes of the world and in the eyes of God. Darlene is in charge of a multimillion dollar project, so she has precious little to give to me either. The communication lines between us become strained.

Instead of talking when we find ourselves alone we argue. What we argue about is sleep. Getting more sleep than the other is like being accused of stealing money. Sometimes of a weekend I sneak into the study and fall asleep on the soft new carpet under my desk. It's the same spot Fergus uses when we play hide and seek. Soon she discovers me. She prods me with her foot, points at her stomach and says, 'If anyone needs more sleep it's me, mister.'

It is also around this time I discovered the soothing delights of red wine. I'd heard other mothers talk about their red or white wine of an evening to calm frazzled nerves. Now, as soon as Fergus is asleep, I am filling a bucket-sized glass with shiraz and gulping it down. The first one feels good but then it starts becoming two to maintain the buzz. I could see how the drinking could get out of control if I keep filling up my wine glass night after night. But the red wine dulls my senses, makes everything bearable. I'm not ready to give it up just yet.

Before Fergus's birth Darlene and I would spend hours discussing the intricacies of our lives. We'd spend afternoons cuddling and watching DVDs like *Sleepless in Seattle* before ordering takeaways. Now there isn't a spare second. Our past life seems a self-indulgent fantasy. I am not able to rub her belly as much now, or sing songs to the unborn baby like I did when she was carrying Fergus. Instead I take to avoidance behaviour, throwing myself into bed as soon as Darlene gets home, thinking, 'If I bury myself under the sheets and say nothing perhaps she won't get upset with me when I ignore her questions about my day with Fergus.' She marches into the bedroom, anyway, turns on the light, starts chatting. Not even Friday night football can save me here.

When twenty weeks have passed and the scans reveal we are having another boy we again break with tradition and name our baby before the birth. Henry had a strong tradition in both our families. My great great-grandfather on my mother's side was called Henry. Grampi's middle name is Henry. The book of baby names Darlene had bought indicated that Henry meant 'ruler of the house'. It would turn out to be an accurate description.

I am asked to give a speech at my father's seventieth birthday, which is going to be held at my sister's place. My siblings hold much the same attitude as me towards my father. All of us, at one time or another, have gone through periods of estrangement with him but for this final act we have agreed to put our grievances aside; to pull together for the display of family unity that Dad so cherishes. We will be *The Brady Bunch*. My older brother tells me that Irish Catholics have a history of pandering to the wishes of a family member who has had the most recent run of bad luck. This would explain why, with death approaching, we are likely to grant him anything.

My father is a skeleton covered in yellowish skin, a skeleton dressed in a cream linen suit and a blue silk shirt. He thinks he looks quite stylish, and he probably would if he was healthy. All I can think of when I look at him is an extra from a Tim Burton movie. His friends are all here, his golfing buddies. I would rather be anywhere other than standing in front of these people, some of whom cannot hide their displeasure at me for not speaking to my father for so many years. One of them had even rung me up not long before and told me that I was a bad son: 'You know, people visit their fathers when they are sent to gaol. And after all he did for you!' I sat on the other end of the phone, silent. He was talking to me like I was a little kid. Like I was still going around to his house for barbeques and to play with his children. Why couldn't I say anything back to defend myself? I hung up quietly while he was still ripping into me.

As I prepare to talk the moment feels impossibly important. One slip and I could shatter the glasshouse I've built around myself. The friend who abused me on the phone is standing there watching me, arms folded across his chest. I'm over-come with a strong urge to explode out of the blocks, to run away down the long driveway of my sister's house. I need to run and run and run to dull the pain until there is nothing left but exhaustion. I should have refused. I should have said no. Why didn't I have the courage to say no? Why couldn't I say, 'Fuck you, Dad, I don't want to play your stupid game anymore.' It's not that the speech has to be perfect but that it has to say all the things people want to hear about the man they love: his humour, his jokes, his love of life, his optimistic attitude. They don't want to hear the real story, the one they don't know, the one about the monster behind the mask. And even if they heard it they wouldn't believe it. If someone told me Andy was a monster who screamed obscenities at his wife and children I wouldn't believe it either.

I'd settled on a topic much loved by my father, whose humour had a self-deprecating edge that made him appear as if he held very few pretensions about himself. As I searched for the right words to say I realised with great relief that Dad had accumulated a spectacular list of accidents that he used to make people laugh at dinner parties and family gatherings. The time he stepped into the shallow end of the Valley Pool during a swimming carnival and five hundred people in the packed stands gave him a standing ovation as he climbed out and gave them the royal wave. The time he drove off with the petrol bowser nozzle still in the Jaguar, which pulled the pump out of the ground and caused a minor state of emergency in the neighbourhood with fire engines, sirens blaring, descending on the scene. The time he slid down a glacier on his backside in Europe, scattering the Austrian Olympic ski team as they prepared for a training run. The time he pulled both hamstring muscles in the father–son race at a school athletics carnival. The time he visited a dentist in Turkey on a whim – he wanted to see how they conducted their business – and stuck his head through the plate-glass door when he was saying goodbye, returning to his hotel with thirty stitches in his head and covered in bandages. It was a relief to know that I didn't really have to say anything about Dad's life, about his terrible behaviour. I didn't have to scratch the surface. All I had to do was retell the old the stories the way I'd heard him tell them, acting much the same way as a puppet. And they love it, just as much as they love him. All these people are dabbing at their eyes. The friend who told me on the phone that I was a bad son is crying, blowing his nose with a hanky.

'Thank you for the gift of laughter, Dad,' I say before sitting down. Dad hugs me. In front of all those people I lower my defences and invite him in, again. I can feel his sharp shoulder blades pushing through his fleshless back into my forearms as I return his embrace. It doesn't feel nearly as bad as I thought it would.

'I love you,' Dad whispers in my ear. I can't bring myself to say anything in return.

The last time I see my father alive we are sitting on his leather couch and when he gets up there is a thin dribble of shit that has leaked out of his pyjamas. He can't eat solid food anymore. He survives on a protein-laden brown liquid that he gets from a tin. The brown liquid has the texture of chocolate topping but smells like the food in a nursing home, bland and horrible. The nurse on the afternoon shift has left for the day and we are waiting for her evening replacement. The father–son bond between us is strengthening again, just like it was when I was younger and worshipped him. I find myself once again enjoy-ing his praise, his corny jokes. *My dog has no nose. How does it smell? Awful.* I'm impressed at the bravery he's showing in the face of death. I keep bracing myself for the angry barbs. They never come.

We had a lovely day together when Dad took Fergus and me to his golf club. We moved around in a cart for nine holes while I hit some shots and Fergus ran about the open fairways. Dad was too sick and tired to play but the fresh air seemed to revive him and he found the energy to hit a chip shot to one of the greens and knock in a putt. As we drove around I thought about some of the good memories. Once when I was a kid I'd fallen off the driveway at a friend's house and cut my leg open on a garden stake, which had taken a huge gash out of the inner thigh of my skinny five-year-old left leg. I remember Dad's hands holding the wound closed and the blood and fat oozing out, him whispering in my ear that it would be okay and that he would never let any harm come to me. He held me tightly as the doctor jabbed the wound with a huge needle and sewed it up. I don't remember the pain, I just remember that I loved being near to Dad, smelling his aftershave, being held close, being safe. I remember at a picnic at Slaughter Falls at the bottom of Mt Coot-Tha playing a game where he'd pretended he was a log and all the kids sat on his back until he started growling like a bear. Then we ran away until he scooped us up and tickled us under the arms. Amid the screams and giggles I really did think my dad was the best in the world.

Some Friday nights while I was in junior school he would present me with a Smurf that he'd purchased from the BP service station opposite his dental surgery. I'd listen for the sounds of his car coming down the driveway and hope there would be a new one in his briefcase to give me after he had his dinner. On special occasions he'd take us all to Gino's restaurant in New Farm on the way to the airport. This was where I tried spaghetti carbonara for the first time. Afterwards there was tartufo for dessert, a ball of ice-cream with hard chocolate on the outside and vanilla and peppermint on the inside. He even let me have a Coke, which was a rare treat indeed for the son of a dentist. He would tell us amazing stories at night, about a prince who flew to our house in a chariot drawn by flying swans. The swans would do a poo on the roof of the neighbours who played their musical instruments too loud and annoyed him. He would describe it as 'drop a little message' and it was only when I was older that I worked out what he really meant. He would put us in the stories and we'd be the ones in the magical land where the prince lived battling monsters and baddies, especially the Giant Blue Jelly Monster. So it wasn't all horrible.

If only I could wipe away the bad memories, press the erase button. If only they could cancel each other out. Perhaps I got it wrong. Perhaps he was a brilliant dad after all.

I look at the mess from Dad's pyjamas and think I should be getting home and giving Fergus his dinner. If I don't go soon he'll probably fall asleep in the car on the way home and that will screw up our whole routine. Instead of going I clean up the shit with one of the baby wipes in my nappy bag. I place the wipe into a deodorised bag and put it in the bin. Just like I have to do with Fergus when he is sick, I dress Dad in clean pyjamas, and then I give him his medicine. He chugs down several large ominous-looking tablets. A friend whose father had cancer couldn't resist taking one of his father's morphine pills. He couldn't feel his legs and collapsed at the pub and they had to call an ambulance. Dad is taking bucketloads of morphine yet he is still able to shuffle around, even catch a plane up north to visit my older brother's beach house near Port Douglas. He has the constitution of an ox, a stomach of iron. In a way I'm looking after two children, one I love with all my heart, and the other I've forgotten how to love or even why I love him.

'He didn't try you know,' Dad says, looking at me with enormous eyes.

'What are you talking about, Dad?' I ask as I tuck him in, pulling the sheet up around his neck.

'My father, he didn't try to save himself when he drowned. He just let the waves wash over him; smash him into the rocks.'

I'd never heard my father talk about the time his father had died. His mother, my grandmother, had forbidden the children from speaking about the drowning. They got on with life as if it had never happened. Dad's father, my grandfather Alan, had taken his two sons, Dad and my uncle Ian, down to Point Lookout on Stradbroke Island to fish. My grandfather Alan was a medic in the Great War. He'd been a lieutenant in the Light Horse field ambulance, awarded a medal for bravery, mentioned in dispatches for helping evacuate wounded diggers under fire in the Middle East around the time of the famous charge of Beersheba. At Point Lookout, he'd lowered himself onto the rocks to untangle a fishing line when a rogue wave washed him into the ocean, which was started to boil as a storm approached.

'He looked at me and it was almost like he was smiling, and then he was gone,' Dad continues. 'When we told Mum that Dad was missing she collapsed in the kitchen. She made a sound that was barely human, like a dog moaning. She stayed like that for ages, just lying there moaning. I tried to pick her up but I couldn't.' Grandfather Alan's body was never found.

Dad starts weeping and I realise that I've never seen my dad cry before. He was either happy or angry. There was nothing in-between, no emotional middle ground.

'It's okay, Dad, you don't have to tell me this. It's just making you upset.'

'You know I'm looking forward to meeting Dad again and asking him why he didn't try.'

The drugs start to kick in and Dad closes his eyes and drifts off to sleep. The nurse arrives to begin her shift. Fergus is sitting on my lap. I give Fergus a hug and hold him close to me, holding my nose in the crook of his neck and breathing in his wonderful childish smell. I want him to mask the smell of death coming from my father beside me. For the first time I need my son more than he needs me. I never doubted that Dad loved me but perhaps the love was sucked out of him much the same way his father had been sucked out to sea. It was almost as though Dad's concept of love was learned by reading books or watching movies. He said all the right things when the mood took him but there was a woodenness to his actions, as if he didn't feel what he was saying. Perhaps he really is a hollow man. He desperately seeks affection but doesn't know how to return it. I think about the ten-year-old boy who watched his father drown. Who watched his mother moaning on the floor. Who was forbidden from ever speaking about the subject. Should I forgive him for the way he acted? Was it his fault at all that he'd never learned to control his emotions, that he'd never learned how to love?

A few days later the doctor puts Dad on a drip to ease the pain. My father is incoherent when I come to visit and is mumbling strange sentences as he goes in and out of consciousness.

I am sitting at his bedside with Fergus on my knee, trying to find the words to say because I know that it's all over, it's just a matter of time. The doctor has said as much.

'Goodbye, Dad,' I say giving him a kiss on the forehead. He reaches out and grabs me by the neck, pulls me close to him.

'You've made me so happy.' The words are clear and loud but I wonder if he actually said them at all, that maybe I imagined it, because now he is babbling away again making no sense at all. He mentions something about a nun who hit him with a school bell. There is a nurse outside his bedroom. She had heard what Dad has said to me.

'That was wonderful,' she says going all misty eyed. All I can think is he has said the very thing that every son would want to hear when their father is dying. But why does it piss me off so much? *Well that's just fucking great, I made you so happy but you made me so miserable.* I'm not going to cry. Deep down somewhere I know the metaphorical storm is approaching, that there has to be some sort of retribution to all this confusion and pain and anger. I am a dam in the drought, waiting for the rains to come.

When we were little Dad took us three boys to the ski fields at Falls Creek. Mum stayed at home with my sister. We drove all the way to Victoria from Brisbane. It took over a week and in that journey he played just three tapes: Max Bygraves greatest hits, The Andrews Sisters greatest hits and Hank Williams greatest hits. I think there is something in the Geneva

Convention against playing those tapes to prisoners of war let alone to small children. A few nights after I had cleaned up the shit my younger brother phoned and said Dad had the death rattle, his breathing was slow and laboured, sounding like a tennis ball let loose in a metal drum. Daniel said Dad was listening to that Hank Williams' song we all hated: 'I went down to the river to watch the fish swim by . . . but the doggone river was dry.'

And then he died.

I drive through the vacant streets because it is close to midnight. The air seems charged with electricity, like I'm in a slot car attached to a power point – I'm hardly aware that I'm the one driving it, making the decisions. Outside as I park the car I can't remember much about how I got there, as if I've travelled from point A to point B by clicking my fingers. When I get to him he is lying in the bedroom of his unit, arms crossed over his chest and a towel under his chin to stop his mouth from falling open. The lips are thin, still twisted in a kind of painful grimace, and his eyes have rolled back into his head. As a journalist I have seen dead bodies in all kinds of settings but this is different, there is an intimacy that washes over me with a horrible aching groan. I stroke my father's hair and lean down to kiss his forehead. I sense emptiness to the body, a departed energy. Could it be that his spirit has flown away outside the unit and is now zooming around the Story Bridge? Perhaps he's in heaven already, chatting to his dad. Or maybe his soul, if he had one, has been confined to the bowels of hell, which by the look of pain on his face is a real possibility. I kiss my father one more time and walk outside where my younger brother and his girlfriend are waiting.

I think about Dad's eyes rolled back in his head and his twisted grimace. I go back in again and close the eyes properly and readjust the towel so the mouth is closed. I kiss his forehead again. I couldn't stand the sight of him before and now I can't stop touching him. He looks more peaceful, though, and it's a better last image to have in my mind, a much better mental photo. The doctor has signed the death certificate and soon two men dressed in black and looking suitably sombre arrive from the funeral parlour. They look like they have come straight from central casting and act just the way undertakers are meant to act. As they pick up his body to place it in the black bag one of them slips and they struggle not to drop him on the carpet. Then the lead undertaker smashes his shin on the edge of the bed. I could tell he wanted to grab his shin and hop around the floor in pain, was probably missing a huge chunk of skin and was feeling the blood trickle down into his shoe, but given the circumstances with our family's eyes watching him he could not cry out, suffering in reserved silence.

Dad would have loved it, pure slapstick, just like something out of Monty Python. I remember Dad and I watching the famous scene from *The Holy Grail* where the black knight gets his limbs chopped off one after the other in a sword fight with King Arthur. Finally reduced to a bloody torso, the black knight yells out that King Arthur is a coward for not wanting to fight on or at the very least calling it a draw. The blood spurting out in crimson streams shocked me and I was still too young to understand why Dad found it so amusing.

'You shouldn't be watching this,' Dad had said. 'Don't ever tell your mother.'

They load Dad onto a trolley and I go with them towards the lift. Next door a party is in full swing with young people dancing and listening to loud music, munching on food, drinking alcohol, and laughing. It didn't seem right that they could be having a party when someone had died just a few metres away from them. but that was what was happening. I want to shout out for the world to stop, just for a second, just to let us get our heads around what was happening, but life goes on – the noise from the party and the gentle hum of the cars on the Story Bridge continuing on as it always does.

It seems to take forever for the lift doors to open and close but this felt like I had gotten my wish – the world stopped for we didn't see anyone when we went down into the building's basement and car park, when normally you would see dozens of people at that time of night, especially when a party was in full swing. They load him into the back of the hearse and I click the buzzer to let them out of the garage. As the gate rattles Dad is driven away by two strange men from K.M. Smith, one of whom is probably only now letting out a wail of pain, rubbing and clutching at his shin.

★

Fergus is wriggling about on the change table and refusing to let me put on his pants and shoes. Every time I get one leg in his pants he contorts his body and it slips out again.

'Come on, Fergus, please don't be difficult. Not today of all days.' I have spent enough time at home with him now to know that children seem to sense the anxiousness in our voices or through our body language. It is cruel of them I know, but this is when they usually start acting up, when they can sense our distress, the moment when we are losing control.

'No,' Fergus says screwing up his face. 'No, no, no.' I'm dressed in a black suit for the funeral and the tie feels uncomfortably tight about my neck. Since I gave up work to look after Fergus it's been years since I put on a suit. It is August but quite hot. The air conditioner in the house is on the blink and I'm thinking over and over again that I must ring the real estate agent and have it fixed. Focusing on that means I don't have to focus on what this day really means and what's really important. Sweat is trickling down my neck. The grandchildren in the family are being looked after by various babysitters we have hired so we can go to the funeral. I have decided that I will speak at the funeral, not the eulogy, which will be done by my brothers. One last time and then it will be over. That morning I got up and wrote a poem that had been bouncing around in my head all night, almost writing itself. I am not one for writing poetry so this urge comes as quite a surprise. Nor am I one for reading my musings aloud in public. Nevertheless the poem is printed out on a piece of white A4 paper, folded in my pocket, just in case I find the courage.

Some items representing Dad's life are placed on a table towards the back of the church near the altar. I stand at the lectern and explain to the mourners what they signify: a picture of his school, a favourite golf club, a picture of his family taken a few months before by a professional photographer. I tell the mourners that Dad had a flat golf swing and that some of his friends called him the Babe Ruth of golf. I said that if you wanted someone to putt for your life, Dad was one of them, for he had a fierce competitive spirit. He made them when they counted. When my uncle Ian gets up to speak he says it is ironic Dad was known as the Babe Ruth of golf because at the University of Queensland he was called the Jack Nicklaus of baseball. I wondered if he is thinking about the day they watched their father being washed away from the rocks and into the sea. He has battled the black dog of depression all his life. Later he will be trembling as he throws dirt on Dad's coffin as it is lowered into the ground. A few months later he will be dead too.

I am about to sit back down when I remember my poem. I look over the congregation. They stare back at me, the faces of family and friends all blending into one. Nick had said to me before I went into the church, 'It would have been easier for you not to come than to come.' But here I am.

I remember the feeling . . . the smell of Coppertone on
your shoulders as you carried me into the surf . . . waves
crashing . . . never breaking stride . . . a colossus
No relationship is perfect but there were times when you
and I came as close as father and son could . . .

A raw powerful sadness overwhelms me as I'm standing there. The words go fuzzy, and my legs and arms start to tremble. I look around at the priest and then at heavily pregnant Darlene in the front row because I'm expecting them to come towards me and take me back to my seat – it must be obvious to them I can't go on. I look at the gold handles on the coffin and the flowers placed upon the dark brown wood and I can't imagine that he is lying in there – it's better to think that his spirit is zipping around the church, perhaps sitting in the cloisters watching proceedings unfold. He would be impressed by the tenor and soprano we have hired from Opera Queensland to sing 'Ava Maria'. I'm standing there frozen, and it's like I've been standing there for an hour even thought it's only a second. My thoughts are trapped in a prism of white light. There is no one else in the church now; it's just Dad and me. I hear his voice, all-consuming, throbbing through me as though it's crept into every crevice, not just in my head.

'You're not trying hard enough,' he says. And that's when the tears start.

They stream down my face and I have a breathless sobbing tone to my voice that I find embarrassing. But it feels good to cry, to release the valve. And out it all comes, a son's love for his father.

'I remember,' I say quietly, before heading back to my seat.

9

RELAX, STAY CALM

Darlene is past her due date. The obstetrician has recommended another Caesarean section as the scar from the previous operation is in danger of rupturing. Her stomach seems bigger than last time, pointed at the end like a hard-boiled egg. Prepped for surgery she is wheeled into a quiet corner off the operating room. Once again, I'm dressed in my light-blue shower cap and gown and I am sitting beside her, wringing my hands with worry, occasionally standing up to pace around. The panic attacks that started at the car dealership a few weeks earlier have now taken a firm grip on me and it's all I can do to not grab a brown paper bag at every opportunity to stop myself from hyperventilating.

My older brother was left the responsibility of managing Dad's estate. My older brother used to put Dad's toothbrush in the toilet and flush water over the bristles when Dad had yelled at him. I thought my trick with the green ants was much more inventive.

'He left most of it to Mum,' he told me over the phone from Melbourne where he lives. My older brother, despite falling on his head several times as a child, is a successful industrial designer with a flourishing business.

'Why would he do that? They're divorced.'

'He always loved her,' he said. Which is true. When Dad was dying, when his breath had a guttural edge to it with the air going out and not being sucked back in, Mum had whispered to him, 'It's okay to let go.' When he still fought on she whispered to him again, 'I love you.' That was when he gave up. So it wasn't Hank Williams that killed him after all. Did she really mean it? I didn't have the heart to ask her because I didn't want to know the answer.

'What do you want me to do?'

'I want you to sell the Mercedes-Benz.'

I had tried to sell the car, but things had not got off to a good start. The dealer who sold Dad the car for a quarter of a million dollars just two months previously was now offering to buy it back for ninety thousand. Dad had only driven it a handful of times, usually dangerously as he was drugged to the eyeballs.

'My father told you he was dying,' I said. 'He told my brother that you would buy it back for a fair price.'

'This is a fair price,' he replied. 'These cars are not easy to sell.'

I told him he had taken advantage of a terminally ill man who was on medication and that I was considering legal action. He wouldn't budge and just sat there with a stupid smirk on his face. I told him my younger brother was a barrister, which sounded much more threatening than me telling him I'm a stay-at-home dad. He shifted in his seat.

'We'll see what we can do.'

He went away and spoke to the manager. They stand in another cubicle with glass walls and I could see them both waving their arms around in animated gestures, putting on a show. The dealer came back. The price went up ten thousand.

'Our final offer,' he said.

I looked at the car dealer and I was thinking about the millions of ways I could have wiped that smug smile off his face. *Double, double toil and trouble . . .* But then it occurred to me that there was absolutely no reason I should be there doing this. *I don't want to be angry anymore. I am not like him. I would never be like him. I've my own family to look after, a pregnant wife and a toddler who need me. I've done enough.*

I sat there drowning in old painful memories, gasping for breath. *Haven't I done enough? He's dead and it's over.* This realisation registered and my mouth went dry, bone dry, like I'd swallowed a mouthful of sand. Adrenalin shot down my arms and legs, followed by the strong urge to vomit. There were no blocks to explode out of. No race to win. All I could do was sit there, helpless. My head swam with blood as a line of sweat beaded across my forehead. There was a sense of impending doom as my heart thumped violently in my chest. *Get out! Get out! You are going to stop breathing.*

I leaned forward on the desk, trying to look like I was going to say something important, but all I was thinking about was how to get some air into my lungs. *What the fuck is happening to me? Get out! Get out!* The voice in my head, the little man, was screaming.

The car dealer clutched nervously at his tie as I found the composure to pour myself a glass of water. He could see that my hands were shaking. Somehow I sensed that if I got up and ran then the terrible panic I was feeling would never stop, that I would be running for the rest of my life.

'You'll be hearing from me,' I said, standing up.

But he never did.

You're going to pass out. You must get out of here. The obstetrician appears, pulling back the curtain just as my fear of enclosed spaces is getting the better of me. He apologises for the slight delay and says we won't have long to wait.

'It's almost show time,' he tells us. As he's speaking I look down at his feet and am surprised to see he's wearing blood-spattered galoshes.

'Everything okay?' he asks Darlene.

'Nervous and excited,' she says.

'And what about you?' he says to me. 'You looking forward to being a father again?'

'Absolutely,' I say trying to sound confident. What would

he have said if I'd told him the truth? That no, I'm not looking forward to being a father again. I am terrified. I am terrified that one day I won't be able to control the anger. What would he have done if I'd broken down in his arms saying, 'I can't take it anymore, Doc, I can't take it.' He strolls away and I can hear his galoshes squeaking across the shiny white floor.

A few minutes later a hospital orderly appears and wheels Darlene's bed under the bright lights of the operating theatre.

'Are you okay, you look a bit pale?' the nurse asks me. I see my reflection in the glass windows off the corridor and it shocks me. My face is drained of blood. I look frightened. She grabs a chair and invites me to sit down. And now I am humiliated because I am meant to be here looking after my wife.

My gut instinct is to fight the anxiety, to wrestle with it, to beat it like it was a physical thing, but the harder I fight, the more I want to claim victory over it, the stronger the attacks become. Since the incident at the car dealership my heart has been pounding against my chest day and night. I couldn't breathe when I saw the accountant about a tax return. I could barely speak as the muscles in my neck constricted, reducing me to a coughing fit. *If you don't get out of this room, you are going to die.* A trip to the video store on the weekend produced a similar result. *Get out, get out. You've got to get out of here.* And then there is a crushing feeling of helplessness that seems to have descended on me since Dad died, a black cloak of sadness that is suffocating and numbing.

I had started to think about the various ways I could harm myself: hooking a pipe to the exhaust and turning on the car, taking sleeping pills, hoisting myself from a beam under the house. It was more fantasy than reality but I was becoming convinced my family would be better off without me. I would wake in the mornings and couldn't imagine how I was going to get through the day. The depression had a hefty form that made my shoulders sag. I am annoyed, too, because this was something that happens to other people.

I thought about the articles I'd written for the paper, about celebrities who had spoken about depression. I admired them for their courage but a part of me thought they were weak. I am weak. *How did I let myself get like this?* I am free of my father but now that he is gone I no longer wanted to live anymore. It doesn't make sense.

Darlene smiles and reaches out to grab my hand.

'Here we go,' she says. I take slow, deep breaths and try to relax the muscles in my neck and shoulders because I looked up the Beyond Blue website and that's what the experts say you should do. *Relax. Stay calm. This is all in your head. You can get through this.* Luckily there is a familiarity to the operation that I find somewhat comforting. It is in the same theatre in the same part of the hospital. I understand the order of things and how it will be played out. Would I have coped with all the unpredictability of a natural birth? The anaesthetist this time around is young and tall and confident. He walks like a man who is used to bending down as he passes through doorways. There is no music playing in the background, no

Rolling Stones as he performs the delicate task of injecting the pain-relieving medication into Darlene's spine. As before, she starts shivering from the epidural.

When Henry emerges from the womb the obstetrician shouts, 'He's a bruiser,' and dangles him before me, all bloody and yellow and screaming. The flash from the digital camera jolts me from my dream-like state. Is any of this really happening? I'm a punch-drunk boxer, hanging on the ropes. I cut the umbilical cord and it's just as awkward as I remember, although this time I'm trembling for different reasons. *Breathe in. Breathe out.* All I can think of is that I must get through it.

Henry is nearly ten pounds, or four and half kilograms, and has massive feet. He's tall too, as long as Fergus was.

'You've got a giant on your hands,' the nurse says as she records the measurements. She has a slight accent and looks familiar. The rims of her glasses are bright red.

'I know you,' I say. 'Aren't you from the deli?' I never would have guessed that the owner of our local delicatessen moonlighted as a nurse. She makes lovely turkey and salad sandwiches and a mean flat white. And now she has helped deliver our baby. The realisation distracts me from the battle going on in my mind. I'm glad for the chance to chat because it means I don't have to think about collapsing on the floor.

'Haven't you heard?' she says. 'I've sold the deli.'

Nanna and Grampi have looked after Fergus during Henry's birth. The day after they bring him up to our room at the

Mater Mothers' Hospital. He is dressed in a purple shirt, cream shorts and sucking on his dummy, having a wonderful time with his grandparents who are like all grandparents and let him get away with things he is not allowed to do at home. He has been sipping fizzy drinks and eating cupcakes. He runs around punching the helium balloons of congratulations that are bunched outside the bathroom. I pick him up and cuddle him, relishing the opportunity to hold him in my arms, because holding him gives me strength, holding him gives me a reason to live, to keep going. He smells of No More Tears shampoo and the roses and lilies that Nanna has brought along to brighten up our room.

Darlene has bought him a toy train as a present so he will remember fondly the moment he first meets his brother but more importantly so that he doesn't realise that he is no longer the centre of attention. He ignores the train and grabs the plastic hospital cot where Henry is sleeping and pulls it towards the door.

'Off,' he says and everyone laughs. He also wants to climb up on the bed and give mummy a hug. He doesn't understand why she can't pick him up. He swings himself up and snuggles into her anyway and she grimaces as he bumps into her newly stitched wound.

The GP tells me, 'I think these panic attacks you're having might have something to do with your father's death.'

'You don't say,' I reply.

'The good news,' she says, 'is that there are drugs that can help you get over this little hurdle.'

It feels much more serious than a 'little hurdle', but the doctor tells me this happens to people all the time and the most important thing to remember is that I will get over it and life will return to normal. I don't know what normal is anymore. Is normal running around after small children and getting no sleep? Is normal feeling my heart bursting out of my chest and wanting to throw myself off the Gateway Bridge? She taps away at her computer and on the screen appears a huge list of medications that could be prescribed for people with conditions such as mine. So there it was. The answers to my problems were a pill.

When I was a teenager I'd seen a picture in a magazine of a heroin addict with rotten teeth and a gaunt sunken face, beside which was a photo of the person before they were sick, with glowing healthy skin and a golden smile. I decided then and there, I remember quite clearly, that drugs would not be for me. Why would anyone want to risk doing that much damage to themselves, of wasting away to nothing? The word heroin always terrified me, conjuring up images in my mind, reminding me of the black riders in *The Lord of the Rings*. And then there was that incident in Amsterdam when I freaked out on the hash cookies.

'I think these will be good for you,' the doctor says as she prints out the script. The drugs are called Elfexor. When I try to get off them I find out that in the industry they call them 'side efexor'. I had dizzy spells, nausea and cold sweats, so in the end I became a kind of junkie after all.

The worst part about being on medication of this kind is that I have to take my children into the pharmacy to get the script filled. I feel I am an embarrassment and a failure as a parent. But I know the statistics; there are hundreds of thousands of people out there on these kinds of drugs. The doctor must fill out scripts like this all the time. Over the next few weeks I start looking at other people wondering what hidden ailments are bothering them, what secrets they are not sharing with the world. Did everyone have injustices that one day would tip them over the edge? Andy and Nick are oblivious to my predicament as are my siblings. For the moment I'm holding my cards close to my chest like it's a dirty secret. I pray at night to make it go away. As we're standing at the pharmacy counter Fergus is bugging me for some Pringles he has spotted on a shelf. The Pringles are close enough for him to reach out and pick them up.

'Can I have some chippies, Daddy?'

'Maybe,' I reply.

'Make up your mind, Daddy, yes or no?' His personality is really starting to emerge and he comes out with these statements from time to time, and they astound me. *My baby is growing up.*

'No,' I say. He throws himself on the floor and has a tantrum.

Back at home Henry refuses to sleep. From the moment he is born he seems to be in a perpetual state of frustration, opening up his mouth and wailing at the world. My mother tells me this is a sign of intelligence, which doesn't make us feel any better. If this is true then our baby is obviously an evil genius trying to destroy us through lack of sleep. I watch him and wonder if I am to blame for his behaviour, that somehow my mood swings have rubbed off on him.

Darlene perseveres with the breastfeeding and the mastitis returns again. There are more long hot showers and sleepless nights as I massage out the lumps. One night while I am changing Henry his bottom explodes, covering my pyjamas and the laundry bench in a light-brown shower of shit. Darlene, on hearing my cries, hobbles out of bed clutching her stomach and surveys the damage.

'Oh my god,' she says. I tell her to take a photo of me for posterity, so that one day I can look back and laugh at my predicament. It's also my first real poo story with Henry. Andy and Sally had their Beaudesert Hospital story. Other friends have a daughter who combed poo through the hair of their second youngest. She has also made pancake-sized poo cakes in her little toy oven and invited her parents to taste them. More than anything, though, I need to laugh, I need to throw back my head and grab my belly and laugh and laugh and that photo of me covered in shit seems like the best way to do it.

For the next few months we stumble around like extras in Michael Jackson's *Thriller* video. There is so much work to do that I barely have time to worry about my mental condition, which seems to be deteriorating the more I ignore it. The glasses of red wine of an evening are not helping and when I finish off a bottle one night in quick time to calm my nerves I decide that this must stop because I don't want to throw 'alcoholic' into the mix. Every morning I splash cold water on my face and tell myself that I have to be happy for my sons and for my wife. I stand in front of the mirror and practise smiling. I hold my shoulders back, stand erect, keep my chin up. I have to make it through the day without taking my frustrations out on my family. I switch to survival mode.

To add to the stress of a new baby we have bought a house, a rundown Queenslander with a poinciana tree out the back. The market is moving again and the money we have saved by renting needs to be put to good use. We now have to pack up and move out of the rental property in Ipswich. The wheel has turned full circle as our new home is just a few doors down from where we owned our first house in Brisbane. It is the kind of house I have always dreamed of owning, the sort of house we used to play in when we were kids. Andy's parents had a Queenslander on a large block and there was always heaps of room to kick a footy or play cowboys and Indians. It was where we had a first cigarette together, stealing one from his mother's packet, climbing onto the hot tin roof, sitting on top of the eaves puffing away, taking in the view as the neighbourhood, where we had our adventures, stretched out before us.

Despite all this, the house needs renovating, the move is exhausting, and I'm still struggling to get by. But our home is close to schools and the train line and we figure that we will have more than enough time to fix things up as we go. First we convert the study into a nursery for Henry, using the cot and the same change table we'd borrowed previously from my sister. Fergus has a room next to ours with his own bed that looks as if it was made in a toy shop. It has a rail guard down one side to stop him from rolling out. He loves his new 'big boy' bed and delights in jumping up and down on it at every opportunity. No, I wasn't going to be like other parents and stop him jumping on the bed. I loved hearing him laugh. Hearing him laugh made me smile, and more than anything I needed to smile.

It's only when you have two that you realise how easy it was with one. Fergus, who had only just started sleeping through the night, starts waking up again upon hearing Henry's hungry cries. At all hours of the night the house seems to come alive with high-pitched wailing. The walls throb and pulsate. Some nights I'm convinced I'm losing my mind. Fergus wants his mummy. He times his tantrums to coincide with Darlene's breastfeeds. He climbs out of his bed late at night and fights his way towards her, past my waving arms as I try to explain to him that mummy is busy. This only makes him more determined to get to her. It makes him angry and his face goes red with frustration. 'I don't want you. I WANT MUMMY!' The only thing holding me together, like it always does, is the thought I will not be like *him*. This is my glue, the key to my survival, and it would seem my destruction as well.

Not long after we move I'm running through the front yard of our new home to the car. It's after midnight. Fergus cannot breathe and is going blue in the face. I drive like a madman to the Wesley Hospital, turning around to check on him to make sure he is still breathing. At the hospital the emergency nurse doesn't seem too concerned by his hacking seal-like cough.

''Tis the season,' she says.

'The season for what?'

'For croup,' she says. 'You're the third case tonight.'

A doctor appears after she has taken his temperature and blood pressure. He gives Fergus a steroid injection. He tells me not to worry when Fergus starts to have trouble breathing. He says that sometimes the best thing to do is take him outside. The change in temperature helps. My mum tells me that I used to get croup and that the best way to deal with it is to stand in the bathroom with the hot water running in the shower, fogging up the windows. 'Steam is the answer,' she says. So now I'm really confused.

For the next few nights the steam seems to work when Fergus coughs and gasps for breath. Then at other times I take him out into the backyard and the cold air seems to calm him down too. I remember reading in one of Darlene's baby books that when everything gets too much, when you feel like you're about to lose control, you should take a deep breath and walk outside. I do. Often. And I also think, 'What must the neighbours be thinking?' This only makes things worse for I imagine I can hear the baby's cries echoing down the street.

★

Darlene has less maternity leave this time around because she does not have as many holidays owing. I remember the four and half months of her maternity leave as if I was looking through the lens of a camera on a slow-shutter speed, sort of like dancing at a nightclub with the strobe lights on, one confusing disjointed scene replaced by another. Before she steps into the car to head off to work we hug, long and slow. Whatever we are going through we are going through it together. What could have driven us apart has made us closer. There can be no tears today for she has been promoted.

Darlene's first day back is on a new bigger project with more than thirty employees under her leadership. But she is paying a huge price and is torn between wanting to be at home with her children and juggling the challenges of work. She is a wonderful mother; she has held everything together since Henry was born. Her nurturing and understanding have made a difficult situation bearable. What if the tables had been turned? Would a man be able to provide his wife the love and support that she has me? It is at this moment that I realise that role reversal perhaps doesn't work. Pretend as we might but it feels to me that there is something incredibly unnatural about the situation playing out. Maybe children should be with their mothers. But for us there are bills to be paid, a mortgage now hanging over our heads. For the time being we are trapped in our little social experiment, trapped by circumstance, hampered by the need for money for a better life for our children, until we can work out another way to do it. I've also seen a high-profile journalist on the ABC and mother of two have a breakdown on television while reading the news. Her husband was a stay-at-home dad. She said later that the 'glamorous job, the gorgeous family and the big house with the water views' had taken its toll.

Could this be Darlene's future as well? Were we also guilty of trying to live up to the myth of 'having it all'.

Before I know it I'm standing on the front doorstep watching Darlene drive away. She has a grim look of determination on her face, similar to the face Fergus pulls when he tries to get her attention. I've had a promotion too. In my arms is a wailing, not quite, five-month-old and grabbing furiously at my legs is a two-year-old wanting to be picked up. If I had trouble getting out of my pyjamas before, it's nothing to the challenges that await me now.

Henry, who cannot yet crawl, will only stop crying during the daylight hours if he is strapped to my chest. If I put him down on the ground for even a second he begins to scream. The only rest I get is when I put him in an automatic rocker that swings back and forth, although I have to place a wooden guard rail around it as Fergus will sometimes idle up and whack Henry over the head with a toy or something harder if I'm not watching. Fergus has not taken kindly to his brother's arrival. He doesn't want to share his toys with this new interloper. Otherwise I spend those first few months at home with the two boys walking in an endless loop through the kitchen, the toy room, our bedroom, the lounge room and back again – over and over until he falls asleep. Then, with all the precision of a surgeon, I have to extract him from the baby sling and get him into his cot before his eyes snap open. If I close the door while this procedure is taking place Fergus will start bashing on it demanding to know where I am and why he can't come in.

Like some kind of shell shock the next six months are almost obliterated from my memory except a series of nightmarish scenes of changing nappies, cleaning up shit and wee, making meals, playing games and changing *Roary the Racing Car* DVDs for *Finley the Fire Engine*. There is a show on television that Henry likes called *In the Night Garden*. The show scares me. The creatures are all squishy and make silly noises and have names like Ninky Nonk, Igglepiggle and Upsy Daisy. It looks like it's been imagined and produced by someone on LSD. My heart is still thumping in my chest.

I manage to get Henry into a routine of sorts with three sleeps a day, gradually reducing it to two. Of course, all this extra work with Henry makes it near impossible to get Fergus off to sleep in his room for his afternoon kip, which involves a different routine – giving him a bottle, reading a story, stroking his hair, rubbing his back. Occasionally I will sing him a lullaby that a babysitter used to sing me: *Close your eyes, say good night, the angels are calling, they are calling little children to Sleepy bye land . . . Sleepy bye land is a lovely land, where children go at night . . . you can do everything you like at Sleepy bye land.* Fergus asks me if he can fly a rocket ship in Sleepy bye land and I tell him he can.

'You can swim in a pool of lemonade, have dinosaurs as pets, eat cookies the size of a flying saucer.' He laughs and drifts off to sleep, saying, 'Oh, Daddy, you're so silly.' Instinctively, there is a knowledge that I must shield my condition from my sons. I will be happy, even if I have to put my fingers into my mouth and wrench the corners upwards. More than ever I dance around with my sons during the day, sing silly songs, put funny hats on my head. I read to them at night, run around the backyard with them during the day. We wrestle. I tickle them. At night I make bath time fun by turning out the lights and shining a torch on their faces, pretending they are possums who have somehow gotten into the bath. Sometimes I am a leprechaun looking for gold, granting them wishes. They will not remember their father with slouched shoulders and a hound-dog demeanour. Never. Some days it takes every fibre of my being to pull this off, but if this is a test, then I will pass it with flying colours. At night, though, the demons come. When there are no little eyes watching me the sadness creeps up on me. For Darlene there is not the need for secrecy. I know it's not fair but I save the pain and weaker moments for her.

Sometimes during the day Fergus refuses to sleep and we have a battle of wills as I pick him up and place him back in his bed, careful not to engage him in conservation about the unfairness of it all. Even without dialogue this battle with Fergus initially went on for up to an hour. Fergus refusing to sleep, Fergus hurling curses at me, me picking him up and silently putting him back, Fergus refusing to sleep, Fergus hurling curses at me, me picking him up . . . All throughout I never say a word. *I'm better than you. I will not be like you.*

Some days, though, the only way I can get both boys to sleep is by driving around in the Pajero, which becomes my fortress of solitude. Once the kids are strapped in they will almost certainly fall under the spell of the gentle rumbling of the car engine and the dulcet tones of the family-friendly pop radio station I like to listen to. Fergus has even started reciting the words to some of Bon Jovi's 'Living on a Prayer' and that old love classic 'Jessie Paint a Picture' sung by Joshua Kadison, which was the first time I realised that their brains are like sponges, soaking up the background noise. I didn't mind so much the Bon Jovi and 'Jessie' but then he had started singing 'I'm Gonna Wash that Man Right Outta my Hair', which he'd seen on television when I caught him watching the musical *South Pacific* with Glenn Close. Then one day when he's a bit older he suddenly belts out: 'Scooby, Scooby Doo did a poo, Shaggy thought that it was candy.' I think about Steve Martin in *Parenthood* where his son sings a song in the back seat he's learned at summer camp: 'When you're sliding into third and you do a great big turd . . . diarrhoea . . . diarrhoea.'

'That was money well spent,' Steve Martin says to his wife.

I have no idea where Fergus has learned this Scooby Doo ditty from. Who was responsible for its lodgement in his head? Certainly not 97.3fm with its classic hits from the eighties and nineties. Mainly I drive around aimlessly, up and down the Centenary Highway while my boys sleep. Occasionally I will hear a song by British band Roachford that sends me back to the early days of my relationship with Darlene.

Roachford's *Feel* was her favourite CD and she'd played it all the time in the townhouse she rented near The Strand. I remember walking down with her to the beach at night to take in the twinkling lights around the harbour, looking out to the Coral Sea and the Great Barrier Reef beyond. We'd sit under the palm trees with some spaghetti marinara bought from the Italian bistro down the road. We shared our dreams. We were falling in love. And we really were free, just like the lyrics say in Roachford's hit 'Lay your Love on me'. It's a good memory to have, especially when I'm driving around with two children asleep in their baby capsule and booster seat, but it doesn't mean I long for those days. Despite the difficulties I still wouldn't change a thing. When I look at my children in the rear-view mirror I see their mother's reflection. No matter what I'm doing it comforts me to know that she is always there. Sometimes I play a Paolo Nutini CD that I bought from JB Hi-Fi after hearing Richard Wilkins give it a glowing review on the *Today* show. Paolo was the new Rod Stewart he said, but until then I'd never heard of him. Ever since, if I play one of the songs from his *These Streets* album, I am immediately transported back to those confusing days driving up and down the Centenary Highway – it is my soundtrack to tiredness and isolation.

Moments of boredom are replaced by moments of rapid action. The boys are in the sandpit Darlene bought for them at Target. It's in the shape of a pirate ship. I'm taking the recycling down to the yellow bin outside when Fergus spots me and asks if he can help. He reaches into the bin and slices his hand open on an empty baked bean can, almost as though he has run his hand down the sharp edge of a knife. I watch in morbid fascination as the cut opens up around the meaty part below his thumb, white and pink underneath at first and then blood streaming out, layer upon layer, until it leaks out across the flesh of his palm. I need to get Fergus to the medical centre at Taringa or the emergency department at Wesley Hospital. This is a wound that must surely require stitches! All very well, but there is Henry to bundle into the car as well and he is not going to come so easily. Bandaging a nasty flesh wound on a toddler while wrestling with a baby is something that you wouldn't wish on your worst enemy.

Then there is another trip to the hospital after I notice that Fergus's snoring is becoming laboured as he sleeps. I take him to an ear, nose and throat specialist at Canossa Hospital at Oxley. I have Henry on my lap and Fergus is playing in an area set up for small children. As usual the waiting time to see the doctor stretches out and soon both boys are restless. Fergus rushes down the hallway and before I can catch him he has opened the door to a consulting room. There is a woman on a bench being looked at by a doctor. They both looked startled and shocked when the door flies open and Fergus barges in, with me right behind him. I place my hands over his eyes.

'Sorry,' I say as I close the door again.

For Fergus the visit to the ENT doctor leads to an operation to have his tonsils and adenoids removed. Fergus spends a night at the Mater Children's Hospital with Darlene and I look after Henry. When he comes home I have decorated the house with dinosaur balloons and he gets to eat all the ice-cream he wants. The rest of the week he wakes in pain every night, looking at me like he's been conned.

Amid all these medical incidents the stock market starts to plunge. The stock market had been an important part of my self-confidence. While I wasn't working I was able to impress Darlene with the extra income I was bringing in with my trades. But the good times were over. Around the world the line on the graphs tumbled. I kept thinking about Warren Buffett and his warnings. When the kids were asleep at home I'd turn the computer on and gasp at the huge amounts of money I was losing.

'Hold on,' the experts were saying. 'Things will recover.' But they weren't recovering. Everything was unravelling. Those sub-prime mortgages Andy had talked about were a toxic debt that was crippling the financial system. Margin loans were being called in. Banks were failing overseas. People were losing their houses. And through it all my heart is thumping in my chest. The panic attacks seem to have taken over the entire world.

At a barbecue a friend of Nick's took particular delight in telling me that the acronym for my role is SAHD. Nick is a smart-arse and has smart-arse friends, so I have no excuse for not being mentally prepared, but I wasn't. The truth is

I haven't been mentally prepared for any adult conversation for a while now, as if my brain has been replaced by the gooey messy contents of a baby food jar. I chuckled at this little aside . . . *Yes, how very clever of you to notice that* . . . while something deep inside me curled up and died. I might as well have been kicked in the balls. Was it just a throwaway line or had they really sensed my weakness, my secret? An overwhelming despair has crept into my life these past few years, as though I've jumped on a slippery slope leading nowhere. SAHD seems right. SAHD fits. How did this happen to me? Was it my father's death? Was it the drugs? Does anyone else feel like this when they are stuck at home with the kids?

I'd hoped staying at home with the kids would turn me into a kind of Superman. Was it the boring clothes I was wearing, my widening girth from the constant snacking on *Toy Story* yoghurts and Cruskits smeared with butter and vegemite, of eating everything left on three plates three times a day because you need to show your kids that you shouldn't waste food, or the way I stood sometimes rocking backwards and forwards as if I was still holding a newborn? Ego-crushing moments lurk around every corner when you're a stay-at-home dad. One day Fergus says: 'Mummy's going off to work. You're going nowhere!' He didn't mean it the way it sounds, of course, but that didn't mean it wasn't true. Sometimes it takes the brutal honesty of a child to point out the bleeding obvious.

Fresh in my mind too is the taunt of the perceptive pimply teenager at the local park who shouted to his mates as I walked past, 'Hey, don't women push the prams?' I wanted to give him a clip around the ears, tell him to pull his pants up, put his baseball cap around the right way. Instead I sighed, shook my head in resignation and soldiered on up the hill towards home, the weight of the orange phil&ted's three-wheeler carrying my two sons making my legs wobble. The pram was the only thing keeping me sane. Just like the afternoon arsenic walks with Fergus now I was addicted to them with Henry. I would bundle the two children into the new streamlined pram (Fergus on top, Henry in a special section down below) and power walk around the footpaths, crossing the rail line towards the Brisbane River, traipsing up and down hills, almost to the point of exhaustion. Physical exhaustion through exercise helped numb the ruminations in my head. Plus the kids loved it. Not only did they get fresh air but the gentle bouncing of the inflatable tyres usually sent them straight to sleep. And that, during arsenic hour, is a good thing.

10

I DON'T LIKE MONDAYS

The first blast catches me by surprise, splashing somewhere over my right shoulder, sounding as though someone has poured the contents of a large bucket on to the lino floor. I do not usually brave the local supermarket at 3pm. Surrounded by so many women and their children at the dreaded school pick-up hour makes me self-conscious, my position all the more obvious to those all-seeing and all-knowing female eyes. What else would a man in his mid-thirties be doing in Coles with a baby strapped to his chest and a toddler in his trolley? Unshaven, dressed in a T-shirt, faded jeans and Havaianas thongs, it may as well be tattooed across my forehead: Stay-At-Home Dad.

The splashing noise is followed by a curious warm wet sensation across the back of my neck and then wafting up, the unmistakable smell of curdled milk and cheese. I know that smell, know exactly what it means, and Coles at three o'clock in the afternoon is not the place to smell it. I spin around and survey the damage. Henry, not yet one year old, is facing inwards, his head positioned snugly below my chin, and I fumble for a second to loosen the buttons on the sling to give me the space to lift his head up, to make sure he isn't choking. Henry's skin is pale and clammy, his cheeks drained of colour, but given the spectacular results of his brief illness he seems remarkably happy. As we make eye contact Henry even manages a toothless gummy smile.

'Perhaps that's the worst of it', I think, as blast number two catches me flush on the mouth, ricocheting upwards through my nose and into my fringe. There is another blast, then another . . . *Oh God, please make him stop. He will surely die if he doesn't stop.* Fergus, his legs dangling through the holes in the foldout seat at the back of the trolley, seems fascinated at the scene playing out before him. He is waiting to see how his daddy will react.

'Yukky,' he says.

I try to remain composed. This has always been my greatest fear: making a fool of myself at the supermarket, drawing attention to myself. What am I to do? Proceed to the checkout to pay for my milk and eggs, my bread and cereals, nappies and zinc-based bum creams, acting the whole time as if nothing is amiss, that I'm not really covered head to toe in Henry's vomit.

I am half expecting a siren to go off, 'Code Blue' to be yelled to warn patrons to clear the area. There is a combined look of horror on the faces of the women around me. One mother about my age with blonde hair cut into a bob and three children tangled around her appendages has her mouth open, as if she wants to say something helpful but can't quite find the words. She looks as if she is about to reach out and help me although she does nothing. Her young children look similarly frightened, as if they have just taken in a scene from *The Exorcist*.

I'll never forget the well-dressed grandmother with red lipstick and gold earrings and an environmentally friendly hessian shopping bag, no doubt filled with organic fruit and vegetables and hormone-free chicken. She looked positively furious, her creased forehead and narrow eyes conveying a simple sentiment: *How dare you bring an ill child into the supermarket!* At this moment I am not the helpless man with a pram that female shop attendants sometimes smile at sweetly on trips to buy hair-care products for Darlene at Indooroopilly Shopping Centre – 'These are for my wife, of course,' I say every time, repeating it faithfully like the well-worn line of a joke I know will always get a laugh. Or the man who keeps old couples amused wrestling with Fergus and cuddling Henry while waiting to be served at Medicare. No, in the eyes of this woman I'm a dead-beat dad who risked the health of his child to get the shopping done; a selfish bastard who put his own needs ahead of those of his child.

To save face I think now might be an appropriate time to say something devastatingly clever, a throwaway Oscar Wilde-like quip that would encapsulate my predicament, explaining that Henry would be fine when we got home, which he is because their powers of disintegration are just as great as their powers of recuperation. Nothing would come, my SAHD brain still the mushy goo it always is. I know now why Michael Keaton says in *Mr Mom*, 'My brain is like oatmeal.' Silence. Then, slowly, ever so slowly, I grab Fergus under the arms, lift him out of the trolley, hold Henry to my chest, and back away from the mess. There aren't enough baby wipes in the world let alone my Bjorn Again nappy bag to cope with this disaster.

'Fuck it,' I say quietly, 'I'm outta here.' For once, I let someone else deal with the situation. And that's when I spot that sneaky bastard Peter Maloney standing there in his blue pin-striped business suit and pointy black shoes.

The twenty years since he stole Elizabeth Hoffman away from me while we were at school gone in an instant. It was at a party at Red Hill and Nick's parents were away overseas. Andy had passed out in the main bedroom and I was checking on him to make sure he wasn't about to do a Bon Scott. I wasn't gone five minutes. It couldn't have been more than ten. But that's all the time that he needed to work his magic and whisk her away. Peter looks suave and confident, like he's just finished work early at an investment bank after a day making millions, although it registers in my mind that he is almost bald which kind of makes me happy. He has some kids with him too, a little boy and girl, older than mine, and they are well behaved and perfect and not vomiting on him. Peter Maloney is staring in my direction but I'll never know if he recognised me. I certainly didn't want to talk to him about the good old days. After all, that's what the parents with prams spot in the car park is for – a quick escape.

At first I thought my SAHDness was because the measure of a man's worth is his job, the amount of money he earns, his breadwinning status, all of which I gave up long ago to look after the kids. But now I'm not so sure. I suspect many women experience the same waning confidence when they are stuck at home, and it has nothing to do with paid work or money. Tiredness brings out all your insecurities, squeezes them to the surface so you have no choice but to deal with them. And I'm not talking about tiredness that you get from working at the office. There is a difference. Weeks and months of interrupted sleep and the long days looking after children induce a unique kind of exhaustion. I recognise it in the stressed, tired faces of the mums at the checkout as they fight to keep their children's mitts off the Freddo frogs and the fizzy drinks and the *Dora the Explorer* DVDs and the multitude of other dangerous things placed so expertly within reach of tiny hands. I know what they know: that it doesn't end when you get home from the shops as there is dinner to prepare, baths to be had, pyjamas they do not want to put on, stories to be read and tired monsters who do not want to go to bed. How long this takes depends entirely on the level of your finely honed negotiating skills.

There are times when Nick has looked after his nieces and nephews on weekends.

'Hey, you're on a good wicket, it wasn't so bad!' he says, thinking I was growing too fond of my new-age status as a stay-at-home dad. He has started calling me Mrs Doubtfire, asking me, when the mood takes him, for cookie and muffin recipes. But, you know, I love him for his jibes, for the balance they give my life. You see, he knows women coo and cluck their approval when they hear that I'm a stay-at-home dad. Instinctively he keeps me on firm and stable ground, reminding me that there are others out there that are appalled at the corner I've wedged myself in. What can I say to Nick, though, to make him see the error of his thinking? How can I explain to him that one night's babysitting doesn't prove anything?

Friends have told me about screaming and wrestling bouts with their toddlers that power through to midnight or beyond, fraying nerves, stretching normally placid tempers to breaking point. No wonder *Go the Fuck to Sleep* became a publishing phenomenon. Sally used to put their oldest daughter on a mattress in the hallway and gradually pull it into the bedroom over the course of the evening because that's the only way they could get her to sleep. Before kids I couldn't imagine how such a thing was possible, especially when Sally always seemed to have everything under control, including Andy. Now, all these years later, I understand how it can come to that, just as I've also learned not to be judgmental.

The mornings are equally tough with a range of difficult hurdles to jump, everything from ridiculous breakfast requests – 'I want my honey on my Weet-Bix after the milk not before' – to the dreaded 'I'm not putting on my shoes' routine that toddlers excel at when they sense you urgently want to get out the door. Even that short trip from the front door to the kids' car seats always takes longer than you could possibly imagine. Loaded down with gear for a trip to the park that would put Edmund Hillary's assault on Everest to shame, this is when Murphy's Law rules. It is a kind of parenting twilight zone, home to all manner of accidents and misfortunes. This is when they fall down and hurt themselves demanding the favourite Batman Bandaid that's in a hard-to-get-to cupboard held shut by a plastic lock. When they do a poo in their pants or spill something horrible down the front of their shirt. When the car won't start because a door was left open and the battery has gone flat. Somebody should do a Ph.D. on this phenomenon.

It's hard enough with one child but add another into the mix with their complex sleep, feed and play schedule and you need the patience of a transcendental yogi master to keep your heart rate from looking like a monitor in a hospital emergency department. Your head is foggy from a night of interrupted sleep, dealing with tears and bottle-feeds and wet beds and a toddler who wants to climb into your warm safe sheets because he is having, in his words, 'night mirrors'. There are threats of castration as the debate with Darlene on who is the most tired is conducted in hushed harsh whispers and through clenched teeth so as not to wake Fergus who is now sprawled at an impossible angle across the few spare centimetres of spare space on the bed.

As the sun rises you hear the kookaburras laughing and it's like they are laughing at you, for stretching before you is the long hard road of the stay-at-home-parent day and all its tan-trums, bumps and imperfections with the late afternoon arsenic hour looming menacingly on the horizon just as energy levels are flagging.

'Just how long have mothers been suffering this?' I won-der, their plight ignored by husbands who suspect that staying at home with the kids is a free ticket to laying on the couch, cracking open the Tim Tams and watching *Oprah*? John Lennon told Yoko, 'I didn't know we were doing this to women.' And now even the ever-patient and understand-ing Darlene has started to question what exactly I get up to during the day, casting a critical eye over the messy state of the house of an evening and why I haven't had the time to stack the dishes in the dishwasher. It doesn't seem to register when I explain to her that dirty dishes and unmopped floors seem so unimportant when the whole day has been spent balanced on the edge of potential disaster. Fergus slipped riding his horse-on-a-stick and whacked his head on the edge of the bed. A bull ant somehow got into Henry's nappy and bit him several times. Fergus nearly got run over in the supermarket car park because he wouldn't hold my hand. Henry pulled the freezer door open and now all our food has melted. Fergus put fifty cents in the crack of his bottom and then put it in his mouth. Henry tried to lick the Harpic toilet dispenser hanging on the bowl. Before I can tell her any of this she asks me why I can't follow one of her simple rules, 'Toys must stay in the toy room,' as she picks up a stray Lego piece that seems to have grown legs and snuck under the television cabinet. As she waves the Lego under my nose I tell her that I'd need the disciplinary skills of the Gestapo to enforce that rule day after day. Those toys creep out into the lounge room much like the tide creeps up on the beach of an afternoon.

Of course, there are times when I wouldn't trade my moments at home for anything: when Fergus wraps his arms around me and whispers that he loves me; when Henry sees the absolute joy of life mirrored in something as simple as a butterfly or a bubble blown with detergent floating across the back garden; when the boys laugh splashing each other in the small blow-up swimming pool (which I know I shouldn't have filled up due to the drought); when we fly a kite at the park and Fergus says to me, 'The wind is not doing what I want it to, Daddy,' or when I'm trying to get the knots out of his hair he decides, 'Daddy, I don't want to brush my hair. I don't want to be handsome.' These are the moments I hold onto. These are the moments when I remind myself why I'm doing this. When else will I get to eat lunch with a pirate wearing a patch on his eye and a fake hook on his hand?

'Why do pirates have patches?' Fergus asks.

'Because they were poked in the eye with a sword,' I reply.

'Ah, so that's why they're so angry all the time.'

There are fantastic questions that stop you in your tracks: 'Why don't the windows in our house have windscreen wipers?' Or the time when an older Henry tells me, 'Dad, your breath smells like cupcakes.'

'Thank you, Henry. Cupcakes smell nice.'

'No Daddy, these are very smelly cupcakes.'

Once I said to Fergus that, 'You'll go to the naughty corner if this behaviour continues. You're making Daddy very tense.'

'Oh, I love tents,' says Fergus, 'When are we going camping?'

Or during the inauguration of Barack Obama when the children seem to sense the importance of the occasion – perhaps it's because my attention is focused on the television instead of them – and Fergus asks, 'Who is that man?'

'This is a historic day,' I say. 'This is America's new President.'

'Oh, I love presents,' he tells me.

I have developed a dread for Monday that is more powerful than anything I ever encountered while working, and it's all I can do not to grab Darlene around the ankles as she stands on the porch ready to leave with her briefcase in one hand and her Blackberry in the other, already at her ear. *Please, I'm begging you, please don't leave.* Mondays hang over me like the Sword of Damocles, albeit shaped like Captain Feathersword's fluffy sabre. There is a relentless, boring, monotony to my life and it begins on Monday.

'Sleep,' I want to shout to the world, 'I need more fucking sleep.' There is no time for anything anymore: no exercise, no serious conversation, no trips to the movies on a whim. Spontaneity is a word that has a thick black mark through it in the dictionary of my life. Fantasise as I might but Darlene isn't coming home from work and flicking me on the bum with a tea towel wanting wild passionate sex. Isn't that how role reversal should work? Then I'd be the one pushing her away: 'Cut that out, I'm just too damn tired.' Strangely enough, there is always enormous amounts of time for *The Wiggles* and *Bob the Builder.*

Once, when both kids were asleep on a Monday afternoon, I ate half a kilogram of tiger prawns left over from the weekend out in the backyard on my own. I picked up my sand wedge and chipped some golf balls around the grass, enjoyed the winter sun on my face, the cool blue cooch grass under my toes, the whole time imagining what Andy and Nick were doing at their stressful jobs in the city. *Whose laughing now, suckers?* So what is this emptiness then that snuggles up to me after the kids are asleep at night and I'm waiting for Darlene to come home? This horrible loneliness that has me desperately reaching for a glass of wine or a block of chocolate to fill the void? Can I blame all of this on my father's death?

'Am I happy?' I ask myself. 'Have children made me happy? And why is this the best job in the world – but also the worst?'

When I first started taking the drugs I could feel them moving through my system, changing the hardwiring in my brain. I would sometimes call Darlene at work to tell her I was struggling.

'How do you feel?' Darlene would ask.

'Weird,' I'd say. 'Like I'm on drugs.'

11

I GET IT — I REALLY GET IT

Early one Monday morning I can't get myself out of bed. The drugs have eased the panic attacks but are also leaving me in a perpetual state of almost catatonic tiredness. Once again Darlene shoulders the burden of feeding the kids their breakfast and is running late for work, briefcase and laptop tucked under her arms. She kisses me and goes out the front door.

'You've got to get up. Please promise me you'll get up,' she says worriedly.

I lift my head and see that the kids are playing in the toy room. They are banging around making lots of noise. Just a few more minutes, I think, then I'll get up. I wake up half an hour later. The house is silent. I know that a silent house is trouble and despite my tiredness throw myself out onto the floor in a commando-style roll. The kids could have opened the front door. They could have wandered down the road and be playing among the traffic lights as large trucks roared by. They could have made their way down to the creek. But the kids are not down the street or playing in the creek. Facing me is a scene of such horror that it takes me a few seconds to comprehend.

There is a lovely hard nugget sitting on the couch and several vegemite-like smears down the edges where Henry has wiped his bottom. An empty nappy sits open nearby, ripped off and abandoned as is Henry's style these days. He has also emptied the entire contents of an enormous honey bottle on the remainder of the couch, which is covered in thick sticky goo. He grins at me, the kind of grin that means he knows that he's done something wrong and is using his adorableness to get him out of trouble. I've learned not to smile back at him when he does this.

'Honey, honey . . .' sings Henry, repeating the line from the song that he's heard on Jerry Seinfeld's *Bee Movie*. And now it's even harder not to smile because that was just so damn cute.

I'm standing there taking in the awesome magnificence of a mess. So this is what happens when you can't get out of bed? I have never had much sympathy for drug addicts or people with depression . . . I could never understand why they couldn't get out of bed. Perhaps they would be more motivated if they knew this is what would happen.

Overriding my horror of the mess is my fear for the where-abouts of Fergus. Henry is safe but Fergus could still be on the loose. I didn't have far to go to find him. He is in the kitchen. He has pulled up the stepladder that we use for teeth brushing and is standing at the bench, sleeves rolled up, look-ing quite pleased with himself. He has opened a two-litre bottle of milk, which he has poured into the coffee machine, the liquid spilling over the bench and pooling in great pud-dles on the floorboards, some of which is already splattering onto the concrete below the house. An opened box of Weet-Bix is scattered about the floor. I can feel myself breaking apart, like a tree that has been struck by lightning and split down the middle. I want to smack them on the bottom, put them in the naughty corner for the rest of their lives. But deep down though I know it's my fault. What did I expect from an eighteen-month-old and a three-year-old? In some ways I have got off easy for my tardy behaviour.

'I'm making you a coffee, Daddy,' Fergus says happily. 'I'm making you breakfast.'

I make a call to Andersons carpet cleaning.

'It's an emergency,' I shout. The woman who answers tells me people often say that. I explain to her my situation.

'You know that really does sound like an emergency.' The carpet cleaner comes around. He puts his hands on his hips and whistles through his teeth.

'Your kid's a regular Pro Hart,' he says as he surveys the couch. He works away feverishly for a couple of hours and at the end the furniture looks as good as new. He even offers to

Scotchgard the dining room chairs just in case. The bill comes in at over $300.

'You got the day off?' he asks when he's finished. It amazes me that even after all I've been through, after all this time, I still can't admit to tradesmen that I'm a stay-at-home dad. It takes too much energy, too much explaining. Better to just play along.

'Yeah,' I say.

'Not much of a day off is it, having to mind the kids?'

'You got that right,' I reply.

The whole time I'm praying that he won't ask me what I do for a living. By now I've had numerous exchanges like this with plumbers and electricians and carpenters who come to fix things in the house. Why does being a stay-at-home dad make me feel like I'm a dole bludger who's skipping an interview? Are they more of a man than me? The answer these days is debatable: recently I opened the door to a tree-lopper while wearing a paper crown coloured in with crayon and glitter. I had forgotten to take it off post-playtime with the kids.

I get it. I get it. The tiredness of looking after children sneaks up on you, whoever you are. Day after day, month after month, year after year, the strain of digging deep to stay interested in stick-figure drawings and eating vegetables and successful trips to the toilet, trying not to gag as you stare at a spectacularly smelly poo – 'Daddy, I've done a poo that looks like a chicken drumstick' – while applauding wildly at the same time: 'Well done. Bravo!' – *Actually, it does look like a chicken drumstick.* And just when the kids are asleep of an evening, and the house is finally quiet, you lie on the couch for a bit of *me* time, open the pages of a book or magazine, maybe watch a television show you actually want to watch. Then you hear your partner's car pull up in the driveway.

How is it that they can time their arrival home just when their help is no longer needed? This behaviour seems to have bridged the gap of the sexes for Sally accuses Andy of possessing the same sixth sense. And in they come, sometimes in a rotten mood, wanting to unload about their day at work. The hardest part is when they whinge. You're fed up with whingeing. You've had it up to here with twelve hours of children whingeing. I used to think work was *so* important but now I find it *so* completely boring and *so* unimportant and it's all I can do to stop myself from shouting, 'Well just quit the fucking job then!'

But you nod your head and try to make the right noises because after the day you've had you just want to keep the peace. They realise soon enough that you're not interested because your eyes keep flicking from *Law and Order* back to them, and then you're accused of not being supportive. So you get angry at them, telling them, 'Hey, I've had a pretty full-on day as well,' although you can't quite explain what it is that you've been doing apart from cleaning up shit and wee, rocking babies who scream for hours as the blood vessels in their foreheads start bursting before they finally succumb to the tiredness and go to sleep, and serving a multitude of snacks to rude little customers who never say please or thank you unless you threaten them with the removal of a limb.

Dealing with toddlers is like dealing with ruthless midget businessmen who are constantly searching for signs of weakness to get a better deal, at ways to bend the rules for their express advantage: 'Today is Tuesday. That means I can have two biscuits, doesn't it, Daddy?' It was around this time I busted Henry peeing on his hands after going to the potty. He knew I checked them to make sure he'd washed them under the tap. I could hear his little mind ticking over: *As long as they're wet he won't know the difference.* I also kind of admired him for his ingenuity and his stubborn resistance to my rules, for spotting the loophole. With days filled with such high drama and emotion is it any wonder that at the end of each week I collapse in a heap as if I've just finished a marathon, thankful Darlene will be able to help me on the weekend, until I realise that it's a marathon that never ends?

Even with Darlene's help there is still a routine to maintain and it distresses me when they deviate from it. Plus I have my manly jobs to perform: lawns to be mowed, edges to be whipper snipped, and gutters to be cleaned. None of these happen during the week due to the presence of the two small children in my care who will destroy the house if I turn my back on them for a second. I take quiet refuge in these tasks even though I complain about them to Darlene. It is my secret that I actually love mowing the lawn, doing the edges and even climbing up a ladder to clean the gutters. It gives me the time alone I can't seem to find these days. Who would have thought that there is solace in the loud droning of the Victa mower?

★

We decide that it is time for Fergus to go to childcare. I don't need to make up stories anymore when asked by car salesmen, charter-boat captains or tradesmen what I do for a living as I have obtained some freelance media work. It is a relief to know that I am in possession of a foolproof cover story to deflect the questioning should the nature of my employment ever arise again. I can make casual employment sound like I'm the next Rupert Murdoch. All I need to do now is free up a few hours each week so I can write at my computer. Childcare also sounds like a good option because Fergus is becoming increasingly bored at home. Without regular play dates at a mothers' group I'm concerned about his lack of regular social contact with other children his age. Nanna and my mother have agreed to share the babysitting duties with Henry on a week-on, week-off basis.

I have had Fergus on the waiting list at this particular child-care centre since before he was born. The nice lady from the centre gives me a tour of the facilities and I secure two days a week for Fergus, on a Thursday and a Friday. The fees are expensive. The extra money I will be bringing in will be eaten up by the cost of the childcare. Again I wonder how single working parents are able to make ends meet when everything is stacked against them. The next week I pack the Queensland Reds backpack he loves with sandwiches, fruit and Cruskits, and mark his name on plastic bags in his lunchbox with a Sharpie pen I have bought at the newsagency. I must include in his kit a spare change of clothes and two sheets: a fitted sheet and a sheet to sleep under. He also needs a drink bottle and a wide-brimmed hat with his name clearly marked. Darlene helps me organise these things, especially the sheets.

We both go with him for the drop off on his first day of childcare. When we leave he clings to Darlene and then to me as if we are pieces of driftwood, as if his life depends upon holding onto us as tight as he can, howling for us not to go. It breaks my heart to pry him off me, one hand at a time, to leave him there, all by himself, not knowing anybody. Darlene is inconsolable. 'This is killing me,' she says. 'Why does everything have to be so bloody hard?' I think of the book *Raising Boys*, a present from Uncle Scott, Darlene's brother, when we found out the sex of our firstborn at the twenty-week scan. On the inside cover he had written: *Ben, you can refer to this book whenever you are not quite sure what is 'the next move' to make. Enjoy having a boy! They are awesome.* I have referred to the book, a million-copy bestseller, often. There is one part that particularly caught my attention, under the heading 'Early childcare is not good for boys'. The author recommends not leaving boys at crèches or childcare centres until they are at least three years old as they are prone to separation anxiety and feelings of abandonment. Studies have shown that this can lead to restless behaviour and aggression that can be carried into school. *Working mums are burdened with enough guilt as it is without reading stuff like this,* I thought when I first read it. As I listen to him cry, I try to find comfort in the fact that Fergus *is* three years old and therefore immune to such behaviours, but he is still howling in the playground being comforted by his new teachers as we walk through the gate into the car

park. Are we doing the right thing? Is all my good nurturing work as a stay-at-home dad about to be undone by a few
hours at work? (I needn't have worried; in the afternoon he
will be crying again because he's had so much fun he doesn't
want to go home!) We are about to drive out when we notice
a mother in the car next to ours. Dressed in a dark business
suit, she is about to head off to work. Moments before, I had
seen her reluctantly handing over her baby, only a few months
old. She has her head on the steering wheel, shoulders heav-
ing. She is weeping.

'Daddy, why is your tummy sticking out?' Fergus asks me one
day. It is a good question. The doctor says that getting back
into shape is of critical importance.

'You need to get active,' she told me. I have stopped
walking with the kids because Fergus is too big to stay in
the pram. And all the stress of child-rearing makes it easy to
find comfort in packets of chips, cakes and pastries. I'm not
obese yet, but I could be. Swimming with the kids one day
at my sister's, I caught a peek at myself in the reflection of the
pool fence. The image of flesh tumbling out of board shorts
was truly terrifying. A quick check on the scales at home
confirmed that I had finally hit the tonne, the magical one
hundred kilograms.

'Wow,' I say out loud to myself, looking at the triple digit
as if it were something both wondrous and soul destroying,
like scoring a century in cricket while no one is watching.

Looking after children has turned me into André the Giant. This may explain why the voice-over for Jenny Craig and Lean Cuisine advertisements seems to form a soundtrack to my life. Either that, or simply because the television constantly buzzes away in the background throughout the day as I scurry around after the children. This is also when I notice that there is a conspiracy against men in all the television commercials. The men are depicted as stupid morons who can't do a thing right, marvelling at their wives' ingenuity as they fix the air fresheners to the wall or convince them that they need to take out life insurance or funeral plans. Men can't fix things. Men can't drive. The women all look at each other knowingly. Yes, my husband is a dufus. How long has this been going on?

It is so easy to put on weight when you're at home with kids simply by polishing off all the leftover spaghetti bolognaise on their plates. But one of my tricks to get through the day was to promise myself a treat if I made it through various stages. This was a stage that happened after I'd given up red wine. If I get the kids to sleep I'll have a few pieces of chocolate. If I get them in the bath I'll have an iced coffee. I'll have a piece of cake. Soon I was rewarding myself with all sorts of treats. One day I was praising Henry for his wonderful eating habits.

'Mr Henry eats everything in the world,' I said.

'Daddy's a Mr Henry for chocolate,' he replied.

Sally must have also noticed my spare tyre because she invites me down to her local pool to swim some laps. There is a crèche there for the kids so there is no excuse.

'But I have no togs,' I tell her.

'They sell togs.'

'But . . .'

'No buts, you're coming.'

I arrive at the pool on a Thursday morning and sort out my children, who seem happy enough to run amok with Sally's kids in the crèche, which has several female childcare workers in attendance. Nearby swimmers churn up and down the lanes, the brilliant blue of the pool matched by the magnificence of the cloudless sky overhead. As I stand here, chlorine filling my nostrils, I'm reminded, somewhat nostalgically, of my days as a teenager when I'd swim three or four kilometres in a session before and after school. Afterwards Nick, Andy and I would eat jelly pythons as we waited for our mums to pick us up. Would my muscles remember those glory days after an absence of twenty years?

With my children safely supervised it's time to get my togs sorted out. Ignoring the floral patterns and streamlined cuts that are popular in men's swimming fashion, I choose a more conservative design in dark blue. But in the change room I can barely squeeze into them. I take them off and it's like I'm holding up a gigantic picnic blanket. I go back out to the front counter.

'These are a bit tight, do you have anything in a bigger size?'

'That *is* the biggest size,' the girl says.

Luckily Sally is already in the pool swimming laps under the guidance of the swim coach. I have also paid money to be under the guidance of the swim coach, but first I have to make it out of those change rooms in these togs without anyone seeing me. On a wooden deck by the pool there are mums drinking coffee and eating biscuits. Curse them. They are using the crèche and the café but are not making use of the swimming pool. I decide that if I move fast enough, there won't be enough time for anyone to pass judgment. A blur of bluish material and pale white skin is all they see as I scoot past and dive across the geriatrics in the slower first lane, sending up a plume of water with my dive-bomb. When I resurface I'm happily and safely in lane two, where I am supposed to be.

'There are steps you know,' says one of the swimmers. I pretend not to hear her as I adjust my goggles.

Sally has also invited me around to her mothers' group. It is a very civilised affair. The women are sitting around the table with prawns and avocado for entrée and salmon pasta for lunch, all washed down with some chardonnay. I have brought along a few bottles of Corona beer. Andy and Nick both ring up while I'm there to see how it's going and I tell them that I'm having a beer and eating prawns and that we're about to start pillow fighting.

'I can't believe I'm working and you're having beers with my wife,' Andy says.

One of Sally's friends tells the story about her son and their newborn.

'The house was too quiet,' she says. 'So I went looking for him. I found him in his brother's cot. He's stuck tampons in his ears and in his mouth and in his bottom, the whole pack. He would have killed him with those bloody tampons if I hadn't come along.'

I tell them a story about friends in Sydney. Their son, who is not yet two years old, pointed to a picture of the supermodel Miranda Kerr in the newspaper and says, 'Mummy.' She was, of course, thrilled with this observation. A few more pages into the newspaper and he points at another picture and says, 'Daddy'. He isn't pointing at a picture of Leonardo DiCaprio. He is pointing at a picture of backpacker murderer Ivan Milat.

'I don't look like a serial killer, do I?' my friend asked.

'I can see it,' I said. 'If I picture you in a cowboy hat and holding a rifle there is a vague resemblance.'

At about this time a naked Henry walks up to me, bends over touching his toes, and asks me to wipe his bottom.

'It's always funny when it's not one of your own kids,' says one of the women.

While I'm pleased that I've finally braved a mothers' group I can't help thinking that I am cheating. These women are the wives of my friends. At childcare I am learning to be the only man in the room for morning teas when parents are asked to stay. I find the situation completely overwhelming, sticking out like the proverbial sore thumb. The women are pleasant to me but I'm never really in the mood to socialise. While Darlene would be fostering relationships and organising play dates, I just want to run out the door and go home. I want to stick to the routine I have with Henry. I want to do my own thing. I can't help wonder whether these women would even trust me enough to leave their children alone with a man if I organised a play date at my house. I wouldn't imagine so. There's no way I'd leave Fergus if it was just the husband at home. I can tell the women at childcare want to ask me more about what I do for a living and how I have ended up doing what I'm doing. Just like with tradesmen at home I didn't want to answer any questions.

Darlene has suggested that maybe I find a fathers' group but I don't think I could handle that either. That is what John Lennon wanted to do but men like to hang out with their friends from school, not necessarily with men who might share a similar lifestyle. Men like to hang out with mates they've played football with, gotten drunk with. They like to be themselves, lower the shield, recount old battle stories. John Lennon on the other hand . . . Well, who wouldn't want to hang out with him. With John Lennon it would have been a different story.

My first night out in months ends in disaster. Nick has managed to get a backstage pass to a Powderfinger concert at the Tivoli. The few beers I've had are making my head swim and I can hear my voice getting louder and louder, my movements more animated and exaggerated. I'm losing control. The little man, the voice in my head, my editor if you will, bids me goodnight about midnight and I'm on my own. Nick introduces me to one of the guitarists and for some reason I feel the urge to start making fun of the material in his pants.

'I hear Lycra is making a big comeback,' I say. Strangely enough he seems happy to talk with me about the material in his pants and goes to the bar to get me a beer, coming back to argue with me about the fact that they're not really Lycra.

'Spandex then,' I say.

'He's a stay-at-home dad,' Nick says apologising.

'That makes sense, he looks like one of The Wiggles in that shirt,' the guitarist says, turning around to sign his autograph for a female fan.

There is a commotion of sorts nearby and I realise that Pat Rafter the tennis star is making his way towards us. He wants to talk to the guitarist. There is a strong urge to run to Pat, throw my arms around him, and tell him that I stayed up all night and watched his US Open wins, sympathise with him over that heartbreaking five-set loss to Goran Ivanišević in the Wimbledon final. I want to tell him that I love the Bond's baby jumpsuit and that perhaps, for practical purposes, we should all be wearing jumpsuits, maybe even Lyrca ones while playing tennis. He is after all paid by Bonds to wear their undies. Before I can say anything Nick drags me away.

I wake up curled up in the wardrobe at home. This is an impressive feat as the wardrobe is from IKEA and it is certainly not big enough for me to sleep inside. Nick had had to help me up into the house where Darlene was waiting in her dressing gown. I sleepwalk when I drink too much. Back in my university days I had woken up in all kinds of weird places: the back of a ute outside Café Neon, which didn't impress the owner who dragged me out and punched me in the nose, and, on one particularly memorable evening, in a headlock after wandering around a stranger's backyard where I had started digging a hole, on my hands and knees, much like a dog. On that night the last thing I remember was alighting from a taxi outside my house. The man who had me in a headlock didn't really want a hole dug in his backyard at 2am, especially when I was throwing large amounts of dirt on his car in the process. He called the police who arrived with flashing lights and sirens. I caught a break though when the police took pity on me and drove me home, a distance of about 100m. The younger constable wanted to arrest me and take me back to the watch house but the senior constable was obviously about to finish his shift and didn't want to bother with the paperwork.

'Maybe you could do some landscaping for me,' the senior constable joked. I bought the man who had me in a headlock a carton of beer as an apology. I also gave him money for the damage I had caused to his car. He told me I had scared him and his wife half to death and that I should be ashamed of myself but took the beer and the money anyway.

There is a special kind of hell reserved for people with hangovers who are forced to look after small children. It's winter and I'm in my dressing gown and Ugg boots. Darlene has fed and dressed the children and has headed off to do the grocery shopping. I watch the boys as I play over and over in my head the shocker I was having at the Powderfinger concert. It's at this moment that Henry stands up and tears off his nappy again showering the room with tiny pebbles of shit, one of which hurtles through the air and lands with a plop into my muesli.

I look at the clock. Darlene is still hours away.

★

Further evidence of my precarious mental state surfaces when I give my stamp of approval to the idea of purchasing a dog. I was warned by Andy that the dog question would pop up eventually, as it had with his children. I thought I'd be ready to deflect it. But I wasn't. Perhaps Darlene and I had not quite gotten over the sudden death of our previous dog Austin not long before Fergus was born. And once we had promised Fergus we would get a dog there was no turning back.

Soon we are at the dog breeders and out comes a little fluffy black-and-white bundle of legs and even though we're just there to look we know that we've become attached. On the way home the kids decide to call him Kenny. He's only a small dog, about the size of a poodle. So now I'm stuck at home looking after two children and dog called Kenny that isn't house-trained. Worse still, it's not long before he starts humping the teddy bears and soft toys and then my leg when I'm kneeling at the bath washing the kids' hair.

One night I take him outside to go to the toilet. It's raining and I slip and bounce down each step: bang, bang, bang. As I'm lying on my back on the wet cement I stare up at the grey-black sky with the rain tumbling down.

'This is quite a life you've carved out for yourself,' I think.

12

HEAR ME ROAR

Bursts of intense energy have replaced my debilitating tiredness. The thumping in my chest has disappeared. The anger seems to have washed out of me too. It's all I can do to stop myself whistling happy little tunes as I go about the housework. It seems impossible now I'm feeling better that I could have ever whipped myself into such a state. Perhaps it is because the children are now sleeping through the night. The world seems a much better place when you have had a good night's sleep, something that has evaded both Darlene and me for nearly four long years.

The GP suggests that before I wean myself off the drugs I

should visit a psychiatrist, just to be sure. So this is what it has come to, I think. I have left Fergus and Henry with Nanna under the guise of another business meeting. She has yet to question why these business meetings are not producing any job offers.

In the waiting room at the psychiatrist's I hold a copy of *Woman's Day* over my face so I can't be recognised. I have heard that this particular office is a favourite haunt of Vietnam veterans. A man with a faded tattoo on his forearm sips water in a glass from a nearby cooler. His wife sits next to him. He has his hand on her knee. Was he a Vietnam veteran? Had people thrown red paint on him when he returned from the war?

'Hey, what are you doing here?' It's Andy's sister. She takes off her sunglasses and sits down beside me. She can tell by the look on my face that I'm embarrassed to be recognised.

'Oh yeah, stupid question,' she says.

Out of the office comes a female psychiatrist. It is actually my second trip to the psychiatrist's. The first one I visited was a man who looked completely bored with my problems and didn't take any notes. Plus he looked like Graham Kennedy. I couldn't take seriously a psychiatrist who looked like an old-time comedian. I kept waiting for him to tell me a joke. I also figured women are much better listeners than men and would probably make better psychiatrists, so I asked to be referred to a female.

As I sit there with this new psychiatrist who doesn't remind me of anyone – maybe a little like Kerri-Anne Kennerley – she seems very concerned and makes all the right noises.

'Your father sounds like a narcissist,' she says. I'd never heard anyone describe him as such and it felt good to give some sort of title to his condition. She tells me after our first session that she doesn't think I need to be on the drugs any more either but it would probably be wise to have a few more sessions just to be sure the attacks don't occur again. She also suggests I undergo hypnotherapy. I'm quite excited at the prospect of this. I like the thought of drifting into a peaceful state and not caring about the world around me. It does concern me that the results could be like you see on *The Footy Show*, when they bring in the celebrity hypnotherapists and everyone runs around acting like a chicken.

'Don't worry, it's nothing like those guys you see on television,' she says.

'This woman's good,' I think. 'She's already reading my mind.'

My first hypnotherapy session does not go well. The therapist asks me to find my happy place where I feel comfortable so I can relax. For a start I can't quite take a happy place seriously because it reminds me of *Happy Gilmore* and his happy place. His guru coach advised him to go to it when he needs to relax and sink a putt. In his happy place there is a beautiful maiden in white lingerie serving him jugs of beer while a dwarf in a cowboy outfit rides around on a tricycle. I finally settle on First Point at Noosa National Park where I asked Darlene to marry me. It was a happy place when we walked hand in hand down to the water and watched the sun set. Then I'd taken out a ring. I had prepared a magnificent speech, which I'd committed to memory and practised over and over again, determined to get the words exactly right. But when the time came I couldn't speak, the words instead coming out in an incoherent jumble.

'Are you asking me to marry you?' Darlene asks.

'Yes, yes, that's what I'm trying to do,' I say.

The psychiatrist talks softly and smoothly and guides me into a relaxed state. I feel the tension sliding off me. But halfway through the session I hit a snag when I start thinking about the day Dad yelled at me for being weak after I'd thrown up in the sand. That was when I'd gone down to First Point and sat there looking out to sea, thinking of faraway lands across the ocean where I could be safe and secure. I imagined I was in Narnia just like Peter, Susan, Edmund and Lucy in *The Lion, The Witch and the Wardrobe*. Some days when the yelling was really bad I'd step into my wardrobe at home and hope that I'd end up in that magical land filled with talking animals and centaurs and fawns. I'd get myself all psyched up. *Maybe this time. Maybe this time.* I'd bang my head on the wood at the back and be bitterly disappointed. The snack bar outside the Noosa National Park in those days made the best hamburgers in the world. The best of the best was the Big Wave Burger. I'm thinking of the day Dad had asked my younger brother and me to go to the snack bar to get him a hamburger and chocolate milkshake. On the way back we accidentally dropped his Big Wave Burger on the road. We picked up the steak and the tomato and the beetroot and the lettuce and put the whole thing back together, not bothering too much about the dirt and pieces of bitumen that had stuck to the food. It scared me to think about what he might do if he suspected we'd sabotaged his meal even though it was an accident. As he watched *World Series Cricket* and ate his hamburger he was none the wiser.

'On the count of three you'll be awake, fully conscious of your surroundings,' I heard the psychiatrist say.

'Something happened towards the end, your breathing changed, you started to tighten up.'

'You're right.' I told her about the Big Wave Burger.

'You need to find another happy place,' she said.

There are two things that help save me my sanity when I go off the drugs. I might not have a mothers' group but I discover an indoor play centre and a crèche at a gym in Indooroopilly. It is a place that I retreat to when I'm at my wits end. I am outnumbered by women by about one hundred to one but once I have set up my station with nappy bag, newspaper and cappuccino I can relax for a time while Fergus and Henry expend copious amounts of energy on the play equipment, safe in the knowledge that they cannot escape out the front door, which is guarded by a female attendant and a metal gate with a magnetic latch. The play centre is good for two hours of zone-out time. The gym at Indooroopilly also proves a saviour, although getting the kids ready for the gym and heading out the door requires almost the same effort as actually doing any physical exercise. The gym has a crèche service that caters for babies as young as six weeks. Many of the mums here use it for an hour while they do their Pump, yoga, Pilates and RPM classes or just pound the treadmills or cardio machines. Again I am outnumbered by women but it is a small price to pay. That doesn't mean it isn't without its embarrassments. The owner of the gym sets me up with a fitness program and leaves me to build up a sweat on the Stairmaster. Bolted to the wall in front of me are nine flat-screen televisions showing free-to-air and cable. I plug my earphones into the audio system and channel surf. On *The Oprah Winfrey Show* a so-called love expert is giving the female audience advice on how to keep a man. He calls sex 'the cookie' because everyone loves cookies no matter what kind they are. He says men want three things from a woman: love, support and 'the cookie'. It's at this point that I realise that I'm the only man in the cardio line because the only people laughing whenever he says 'the cookie' are women. Then the love expert says that a man will go elsewhere if he doesn't get these three things from his partner. 'Ladies, be warned, he'll get his cookie from someone else!' None of the women are laughing anymore. Some of them are looking at me suspiciously.

During crèche hours I'm sometimes the only man in the RPM class, where the instructor often yells out, 'Let's work hard so we can have bikini bodies.' 'Do you want a smaller butt or not?' 'This is what you get for drinking too much chardonnay!' Then one day back on the cardio line the owner of the gym tells me a salesman has left some promotional sweatbands at the front counter. He twirls one around in his fingers. 'Hey, Ben, why don't you try it on?' he jokes. 'You know, to celebrate your return to serious exercise.' I don't want to offend the owner of the gym. He's gone out of his way to make me and my children feel welcome. The endorphins from all the exercise are also proving remarkably effective. 'Well what do you know, it suits you,' he says laughing. And that's when Elizabeth Hoffman walks by. All those years since Peter Maloney stole her away from me at Nick's party are vaporised. I'm right back there at *that* party. 'Danger Zone' from the *Top Gun* soundtrack is playing on the stereo. But Elizabeth Hoffman is not back in 1986. She's very much in the present, with a quizzical expression on her face as she looks at the familiar man on the Stairmaster in the Olivia Newton-John headband. And she keeps on walking.

And then the river bursts its banks. The water creeps up to Nanna and Grampi's house and wipes them out. Everywhere people are covered in mud, carrying brooms and shovels and looking to help their neighbours. People who are complete strangers helping them pull the saturated and ruined gyprock from the walls, sweep out the mud from the kitchen and lounge room and use high-pressure hoses on the paths and windows. Mud is everywhere and it is starting to stink. The power of the flood all over Queensland is on show: trucks on top of cars, sheds on top of houses, a woman's body found eighty kilometres from her home at the bottom of the Toowoomba range. A shark is seen swimming down the main street in a suburb in Ipswich.

As the water recedes and the mud dries up Nanna and Grampi have a haunted look about them. Losing everything you've worked hard for will do that to you. How will they get through this disaster? From my experience I know that it's a matter of taking one day at a time, one brick at a time, slowly rebuilding, never thinking too far ahead. Then one day you wake up and the pain is gone.

While I get to work with a high-powered water pressure cleaner Darlene is helping them take their first tentative steps towards healing: organising emergency payments from the government and helping them to think through what needs to be done. They are looking at her with awe and admiration. I can see how much it means to them to have their daughter's support; a daughter's love for her parents.

Later, after spending the day cleaning up, we load the kids in the car and drive home. We will return day after day for a week to try and get the mud out of the house.

'You know, a daughter would be nice,' I say to Darlene.

He is dressed in a button-up green shirt and grey trousers. On his head is a wide-brimmed hat. His socks are pulled up to his knees and his black shoes with their Velcro strap are more like runners. When I started school the shoes were heavy and uncomfortable with thick laces and, if you were lucky, a paw print of a tiger underneath to give you grip in the playground. On my first day at school Andy and I were sent to see Sister Zeta as punishment for playing in the rainforest next to the playground. The rainforest was out of bounds. The bell hadn't even rung for the first class and we were already outside the headmaster's office.

Andy and I had played in the rainforest during the school holidays when we tagged along with our older brothers. We thought we owned the place: all the vines where we played Tarzan, all the chalk rocks which we crushed and turned into gunpowder for our battles with imaginary pirates, all the leaves which we piled together in great clumps and tried to set on fire by rubbing sticks together like we'd seen the Aborigines do on *In The Wild With Harry Butler*. It all belonged to us. A kid from grade two dobbed on us. I can still remember him smiling as we were marched past, his pants pulled up around his armpits and his black hair slicked back like the ratbag informer he was.

'We're going to be expelled,' Andy said miserably.

'And on our very first day,' I replied. I'd never seen Sister Zeta up close. I'd heard tales from Colin and Kylie about what she did to naughty boys and girls. They involved the cane and sore bottoms and detentions and notes home to parents. When she ushered us into her office she didn't have green skin like the witch in *The Wizard of Oz*, as I'd imagined, but her face was all long and pointed. What must have been going through her mind as she stood over us, two little boys half scared out of their minds? She had a kind voice, much softer than how hard she looked. If she had a cane ready to whip us with I never saw it.

'You're sorry, aren't you?' she said. We nodded our heads furiously. 'Well, run along now and don't do it again.' We both burst into tears from the relief.

As we walk we are a family. We are a happy family. I hold Fergus's hand as we head up the road towards school and I wonder what sort of adventures he will get up to today. What memories will he have of his first day at prep? He asks me to grab his blue drink bottle from the webbing of his backpack. His backpack is so heavy he can hardly walk. He takes a swig and wipes the back of his hand across his mouth.

'Ahhhhh,' he says. It's the same thing I do when I take a drink on a hot day after mowing the lawn. What else has he learned from me? What other habits of mine would he take into the schoolyard? Mummy is giving Henry a piggy-back ride. Henry, who has just turned three and attends the local kindergarten, looks with doting eyes at his brother in his brilliant uniform, almost as if he is about to ask him for his autograph.

'Fergus is a big boy now,' he says to me.

'Yes, Henry, and one day you'll be a big boy too!' It seems every day there are incidents that leave me both horrified and struggling to contain myself from fits of laughter. It is these moments that make being a stay-at-home dad so worthwhile.

Like when Fergus came into the lounge room one day with a huge piece of snot coming out of his nostril, almost stretching to the ground.

'Daddy, we have a problem,' he said. Or when Henry tells Fergus that he has two tricks to show him: one where he hangs upside down on the swing and the other where he just hurts himself. Or the time we are doing some craft and Fergus picks up the glue bottle and takes a big sniff.

'That smells good, Daddy.'

Henry has a sharp mind and a wicked sense of humour. At kindy he will tell the teacher that he wants to be a zombie when he grows up. He asks me if he can go to university and study to be a ninja. Once when I put him in the naughty corner he said: 'Daddy, I wish you were extinct.' He is fascinated by *Star Wars* and asks me if Obi-Wan Kenobi has a brother called 'Obi-Two Kenobi'. When I carry him on my shoulders he sometimes farts and laughs and laughs at the hilarity of it all. He blames Kenny for farts he does around the house and for other crimes that he doesn't dare own up to including crayon scribbles on the wall. He's tested me in ways I'd never imagined. Seeing him pee on the iPad will do that to a person. Henry looks at me as he perches on his mother's back. 'Look at the hairs on my arm,' he says. 'My arms are so hairy I'm almost a daddy.' I see the scar on his forehead that has just healed. He'd fallen over and whacked it on the edge of a wall. As I held the wound together I was reminded of my father all those years ago holding the wound in my leg together as I was rushed to the hospital.

Henry's wound was deep and required several stiches. Fergus hid behind the door when the needle was jabbed into the gash. I held Henry still in my arms. I hope he doesn't remember the pain. I hope he remembers that I held him in my arms and whispered into his ear that he was brave, the bravest boy I'd ever seen. I hope he felt safe in my arms, just like I did with my dad all those years ago.

At the school gates there is a traffic controller helping other children and their parents cross the road.

'A lollipop lady,' I say, knowing it will annoy Fergus.

'It's not a lollipop, Dad,' he says. 'It's a sign attached to a stick.'

'How do you know unless you go up and lick it?' I say. He laughs because we have had this conversation a hundred times since we've moved back into the area. He hates it when I tease him but I also know he loves it too.

Fergus puts his bag into the rack after finding the spot where his name is marked in colourful letters. There are hundreds of kids going into classrooms all about us, and hundreds of parents calling out to them, lots of hugs and kisses, lots of teary goodbyes. Darlene and I meet the teacher who asks us to put a name tag on Fergus's chest. Fergus grabs a train from the toy shelf and starts moving it around a track set up by some of the other boys. Will he be happy at school? Have I given him the confidence? He smiles at the other kids who look just as nervous as him.

When it's time for us to go I kiss him on the cheek and he puts his arms around my neck and hugs me. The smell of his new uniform reminds me that this is a fresh beginning, a new start to a new phase of his life.

I think back over the past five years. There's a bond with my children that has been forged through the daily grind of the routine. Whatever adventures we've been through, we've been through them together. All that is about to change with Fergus. His adventures will be with new people, new faces. Events will happen within these school grounds that are beyond my control. And they will shape his life. Have I done a good enough job? Have I prepared him? As we leave him in his classroom and walk back home it comforts me to know that unlike most dads I can truly say that I've been there every step of the way. I've been there when he crawled, when he walked, when he spoke his first words, when he dropped his toy truck into the lilly pilly bushes and was stung six times by some angry black wasps. It was me who put the Stingose on the bites. I was there to kick the football with him, chase him around the backyard as he yelled with delight, pretending I was a giant who liked eating children for afternoon tea. I splashed in the tiny backyard pool with him on the days when it was impossibly hot, squirted water pistols, chased dragonflies with butterfly nets, hunted for doodlebugs in the dirt under the house, watched planes take off at the airport, built sandcastles at the beach, talked about clouds and rain and thunder and lightning and why they needn't be afraid of storms. I told him that thunder was caused by 'ice giants' playing ten-pin bowling in the clouds and the rain was spill-age from their drinks. The lightning was their mummies and daddies turning off the lights. I've taken him to hospital in the middle of the night, held him tight while injections were put into his arm for polio and measles, worrying the whole time that he might have an adverse reaction and never be the same boy again. I've answered his questions on why the sky is blue and who made the world, read stories, changed his clothes, made his bed, washed his sheets, cooked and made him thousands of meals, sung him to sleep. I've sung Rolf Harris's 'Six White Boomers' with him at Christmas time. We've had light-saber fights in the middle of the day pretending we are Jedi knights. We've been happy together and unhappy together. He's told me that he loves me and shouted that he hates me.

Good and bad, it's all there in my stay-at-home-dad head. And I wouldn't change it for anything.

The room darkens as the sonographer gets to work. Fergus and Henry are sitting on chairs next to Darlene as the cold jelly is applied to the bulge in her stomach. The boys have been in a state of high excitement since we told them over dinner a few months earlier that their mummy was going to have a baby. Henry says, 'That's just what I wanted to happen.' Fergus put his hands on his head, opened his mouth as if to say something, then fell off his chair. It's his little trick at the moment, falling down on the ground when he gets excited. But now that the scan is taking place they have lost interest.

The 3D images of the baby kicking its legs and waving its tiny arms are incredible but Fergus is worried that the foetus looks like an alien from cartoon show *Ben 10*. He is more interested in the iPad we've brought along for them, drawing pictures with his finger using the artwork app downloaded from the Apple Store. Henry has discovered his chair spins around like the carousel at Sea World. 'Turn it around for me, Daddy. Turn it around.'

The scan is a lot more detailed than we experienced four years previously when Henry was the star of the show. The consulting room is decked out much like a home theatre. A huge flat-screened TV is mounted on the wall. The ultrasound machine is more compact and more powerful. The images are clearer, the detail stunning. *Is this really happening? Am I really about to become a father again?*

'So, do you want to know the sex?' the sonographer asks.

We nod our heads in anticipation.

Henry has told us repeatedly over the past few weeks that we will be having a girl. He wants to call her Pretty Face. More importantly Darlene's hairdresser is convinced that we will be having a girl. She has been right in predicting the sex of our two previous pregnancies. She is also Italian and everyone knows that Italian women have a gift for such things.

'Do you know what you're looking for?' the sonographer continues.

'Yes,' Darlene says. 'If it's a boy, we know what we're looking for.'

The sonographer pauses for dramatic effect.

'Well, you won't be seeing anything like that because you're having a girl.'

A girl.

The information swims deliciously in my head. A girl. A daughter. A whole new road opens instantly before me, one paved in bricks of pink: new clothes, new schools, braiding hair and Barbie dolls, ballet schools and tap-dancing lessons. It comes as a great relief, now that it is real, that there is no panic in me, no fear of the future and what being a father to a daughter means. My pulse hasn't exploded. There is no apprehension either, only a smug feeling of contented happiness.

Tears are streaming down Darlene's cheeks and I move over and give her a soft kiss on the lips.

'You're happy?' the sonographer asks Darlene nervously.

'Of course,' Darlene says.

'I had a man react very angrily when I told them they were having a girl. He banged his fist and stormed outside. His wife started crying. They wanted a boy.'

'There are no girls on my side of the family,' Darlene says. 'Five boy grandchildren. This girl is going to be a princess.'

The sonographer, feeling the pressure on hearing this news, checks the sex again.

'Of course, we can't give a hundred per cent guarantee, but that's definitely a girl.'

Later the obstetrician comes in and reconfirms the sex.

'Everything looks great. You're having a girl,' the doctor says calmly.

Our first concern before the scan was that the baby was healthy. A girl would have been nice but we were both expecting a boy. It's what we were used to. As a stay-at-home dad I had always felt comfortable handling boys. When they wrestled and tackled each other Darlene sometimes asked me if it was normal for them to be so rough. A girl would be as mysterious to me as the boys were sometimes to her.

As the sonographer finishes her work I stand in the corner and study my wife. She has given up a lot in the raising of her two boys. Role reversal has robbed her of the chance to experience the day-to-day intimacy with her sons. The grind is relentless and exhausting but, as I've discovered, it's those very things that you cherish when the kids are older. Now that they can dress themselves and brush their teeth, get food from the fridge if they're hungry, pour themselves a drink of milk, the hands-on role is greatly diminished. You realise that those moments when they really need you are fleeting. Ever so slowly, they start to drift away.

I used to tell Darlene that she wasn't missing out on anything when she was at work but now I know that that is not necessarily true. Children teach you to live in the moment. They expose your weaknesses and teach you about yourself. They bring chaos but they also bring magic, if you let them. Darlene has been more active in the lives of her two sons than most working men would have been, most probably more than I would have been if the roles had been reversed. She has woken through the night to soothe and comfort them when they've had colds and aches and pains, when they've been scared of the bogeyman. She has taken every opportunity to spend time with them. More often than not she's been there when they needed their mummy. And she has been there for me when I needed her the most too.

It dawns on me as I look at her that my time as a stay-at-home dad has been one of the great achievements of my life. Despite the difficulties along the way I am stronger than I was before. There are days when I know I can handle anything, as if I really am invincible. I'm more patient. More understanding. I might have dangled on the edge but I haven't fallen to pieces. Some people, like that preacher on YouTube, say that I am not a man, but I know that's not true. How could it be? Staying at home with the kids has made me a better man and I didn't have to go off to work to prove it. I have provided for my family in ways that are impossible to measure. That's one of drawbacks to staying at home (what have you achieved with your day?) but it's also one of the strengths. When you add up all those little incidents it gives you a mighty picture of what you've achieved. It's why dads are so proud when they walk their daughters down the aisle. Why mums cry at weddings. They're adding up all those little pieces. And even at this early stage I'm blessed because I've got more pieces than most. None of this would have happened if I hadn't been given the opportunity. But what of Darlene's opportunity? It would seem that she has been the one burdened with the greatest sacrifice. After all, I wanted to be a stay-at-home dad. I didn't go into the role kicking and screaming. She would much rather have gone down the more traditional road if given the chance.

If I had earned more money it would have been easy for her to make that choice.

In the quest to become pregnant again Darlene scaled back her work hours to four days a week. We had taken a hit to our finances but look at the result. We had adjusted. Perhaps she should scale back even further. Perhaps it is time to end the role reversal permanently. While a part of me yearns to return to work there's another part that wants to keep the adventure going, to use the skills I've learnt one last time. I would like to do it again, ride the crazy rollercoaster one more time and this time do it even better. But it can't be at the expense of my wife. There has to be another way.

Darlene grins as the sonographer wraps up the scan. She holds both hands over her belly and whispers to me in the darkness: 'Daddy, we're having a girl.'

EPILOGUE

Now that I am strong again I take my kids to my father's grave. It's mid-September. There's a slight chill in the air even though the midday sun is blazing overhead. It's his birthday. I haven't been back here since the funeral. Not for years. I wanted to wait until I was ready, clear of mind, until I was off the medication. Fergus and Henry are still too young to understand about death and enjoy running around the open spaces between the bronze and granite plaques that sweep in curved manicured rows down the slope of a hill, facing east as is the Christian tradition so resting souls can see the sunrise and the Second Coming. Perhaps my kids shouldn't be here, but nobody seems to care. In fact, this place seems to benefit from their joy of life, soaking it up and throwing it back out through the natural amphitheatre of the cemetery. Other people are milling around putting flowers on fresh plots. Tiny coloured windmills spin about in the breeze on some headstones. One has the image of a young man killed in a motorcycle accident. The tragedy is decades old but the wound is still raw as his family has covered the grave with a small mountain of remembrances. Other plots are forgotten, falling into disrepair.

Fergus and Henry make their way back to me. Dad's grave is covered in a lush layer of grass. There is a green ant nest hidden in the soil, which I think is kind of ironic. The headstone we purchased still looks new and catches the sun's rays. My boys ask me about Grandpa Col. They have not made the connection that he is lying there under the grass, arms folded across his chest, a Tom Watson Ram putter and two golf balls lying beside him in the coffin. We figured he'd need two balls just in case he ran into one of his mates on the practice green in heaven. I told them Grandpa Col was funny and that they would have loved playing with him. Fergus doesn't remember that he did just that but I have a photo for him when he is older that will prove it. I took them to my father's grave because I wanted to prove to myself that I wasn't angry anymore. And I wanted my father to know that I had forgiven him. Plus he hadn't yet met Henry, his newest grandson.

Am I a better father than he was? It seems ridiculous to have even tried. Dad is still my father. He will always be my father. Yes, I'm lucky that I've been given a chance to know my kids better than most. But it's only the start. There is still such a long way to go and even when you're dead it doesn't end. After all, when you're a parent there is no goal line to cross, you never get to do your touchdown dance, never. I turn my back on my sons so they can't see that I am getting upset. But Henry, smart as a whip, catches on like he always does.

'Why are you crying, Daddy?'

'I have a secret for you, Henry. Sometimes you cry when you are happy.'

'Oh Daddy, why did you tell me that? You know I can't keep a secret.'

So this is what better feels like.

ACKNOWLEDGEMENTS

For the purposes of narrative flow and privacy the names of my closest friends have been changed. This in no way diminishes my heart-felt gratitude for all you have done. Unfortunately there could be no literary disguises for my family and in-laws. Thank you for your love and understanding and for agreeing to let me tell the truth, however painful that might be. Thank you also to Alexandra Payne from UQP for believing in me and encouraging me to tell my story, to John Hunter for early feedback and to Joanne Holliman for her support and editing skills. This book would not have been possible without the unconditional love of my wife Darlene. If you meet the right girl and know it in your heart, don't wait six years to marry her! Through good times and bad, every day with you, Darlene, has been a blessing. And finally to our two boys, Fergus and Henry, and a little baby bump yet to be born, who teach me something new every day and are wonderfully oblivious to the mayhem and the magic.